Understanding the New Covenant

I0143286

A RETURNING TO OUR FIRST LOVE

The Naked Apostles
Phil and Colleen Livingston

Published by: The Naked Apostles

WAUCONDA, IL

The Naked Apostles/Phil and Colleen Livingston
304 Barrington Road
Wauconda, IL 60084
www.nakedapostles.org
email: info@nakedapostles.org

Ordering Information:
Quantity sales. Special discounts are available on quantity purchases by corporations, associations, and others. For details, contact the "Special Sales Department" at the address above.

Understanding the New Covenant: *A Returning to our First Love*/The Naked Apostles, Phil and Colleen Livingston. —1st ed..
ISBN 978-0-9960102-2-1

Table of Contents

This book is dedicated to the One who loves us, Jesus, even though we are undeserving. May the reality and truth of what He did be reflected in this book so that all who read it understand Him, His gift, and how to take advantage of it.

"I will put a new spirit in you. I will put My Spirit within you and cause you to walk in My statutes, and you shall heed My ordinances and do them."

— Ezekiel 36:26-27 Amplified Bible

CHAPTER 1

The Laws of God

NAS JN 1:17 *For the Law was given through Moses; grace and truth were realized through Jesus Christ.*

Moses:

The Ten Commandments

NIV Ex 20:2 *"I am the LORD your God, who brought you out of Egypt, out of the land of slavery.*

NIV Ex 20:3 *"You shall have no other gods before me.*

NIV Ex 20:4 *"You shall not make for yourself an idol in the form of anything in heaven above or on the earth beneath or in the waters below.*

NIV Ex 20:5 *You shall not bow down to them or worship them; for I, the LORD your God, am a jealous God, punishing the children for the sin of the fathers to the third and fourth generation of those who hate me,*

NIV Ex 20:6 *but showing love to a thousand generations of those who love me and keep my commandments.*

NIV Ex 20:7 *"You shall not misuse the name of the LORD your God, for the LORD will not hold anyone guiltless who misuses his name.*

NIV Ex 20:8 *"Remember the Sabbath day by keeping it holy.*

NIV Ex 20:9 *Six days you shall labor and do all your work,*

NIV Ex 20:10 *but the seventh day is a Sabbath to the LORD your God. On it you shall not do any work, neither you, nor your son or daughter, nor your manservant or maidservant, nor your animals, nor the alien within your gates.*

NIV Ex 20:11 For in six days the LORD made the heavens and the earth, the sea, and all that is in them, but he rested on the seventh day. Therefore the LORD blessed the Sabbath day and made it holy.

NIV Ex 20:12 "Honor your father and your mother, so that you may live long in the land the LORD your God is giving you.

NIV Ex 20:13 "You shall not murder.

NIV Ex 20:14 "You shall not commit adultery.

NIV Ex 20:15 "You shall not steal.

NIV Ex 20:16 "You shall not give false testimony against your neighbor.

NIV Ex 20:17 "You shall not covet your neighbor's house. You shall not covet your neighbor's wife, or his manservant or maidservant, his ox or donkey, or anything that belongs to your neighbor."

NIV Mk 12:28 One of the teachers of the law came and heard them debating. Noticing that Jesus had given them a good answer, he asked him, "Of all the commandments, which is the most important?"

NIV Mk 12:29 "The most important one," answered Jesus, "is this: 'Hear, O Israel, the Lord our God, the Lord is one.

NIV Mk 12:30 Love the Lord your God with all your heart and with all your soul and with all your mind and with all your strength.'

NIV Mk 12:31 The second is this: 'Love your neighbor as yourself.' There is no commandment greater than these."

NIV Mt 22:40 All the Law and the Prophets hang on these two commandments."

Moses brought us a code of behavior. Within is a spiritual aspect to those codes of behavior. This is because these commands are given to the whole man by God (whom about Jesus says, "God is Spirit"). As a part of the whole man's nature he has a spirit and a soul (mind) which is clothed in a physical embodiment. Although the body functions in the physical world, it is not the only world the whole man functions in and has a cause and effect relationship with.

The spirit realm is the other world that his invisible natures have a relationship with. We live life simultaneously in two different worlds, having a cause and effect relationship with both of these worlds. Being unspiritual as we are, our awareness is almost exclusively focused on the relationship our body has with its natural world. As such, we only concern ourselves with what things mean to us in the natural world. This holds true with the laws given to us by God through Moses. We only relate to those laws in an unspiritual way. This means we interpret them according to how we should conduct ourselves in an outward behavioral way. We focus our concern on obeying the laws in that respect. All while the spiritual aspect to the same laws go all but completely ignored and not complied with.

Let us look at the Law's spiritual aspect. The first and the last of the commandments, for example, are decidedly spiritual, which gives all the commandments in between a spiritual aspect. The first commandment, to love the Lord your God with all your heart and with all your soul and with all your mind and with all your strength, is to interact with the Lord with the whole of one's being. By nature of the command, it is not a superficial interaction honored with merely outward deeds. It demands much more. To be in line with the manner it prescribes is both an outward and inward (or spiritual) conformity to God. For the man who loves God in the manner this commandment demands causes God to be perceived as the beginning and end of all things and the center of all things, with everything revolving around and conforming to His purposes and will before one's own will.

In the United States justice system there are laws against fraud. Fraud is committed when one purposely deceives and cheats someone out of something for personal gain. However, in the law fraud is considered an intent. And as a result, when one is charged with fraud it has to be proven that there was a purposeful intent or motive to unfairly cheat someone out of something before one can be convicted of such a crime.

For example, an individual writes a bad check in the course of buying something. The creditor, in his attempt to get his due, files charges against the check writer for the crime of check fraud. Most people are unaware of this, however, in our justice system it is not enough that someone wrote a bad check for them to be found guilty of check fraud, thereby making them subject to having committed a crime. It must be proven that the check writer wrote that bad check knowing he did not have an ability to pay and intended to cheat his victim. If the bad check was a matter of an oversight, a bookkeeping error, or it happened as a result of an unforeseen loss on his part (like unexpected funds taken from his account), then the check writer cannot be found guilty of check fraud, even if he continues to be unable to pay back the balance.

To be found guilty of fraud, an intent has to be established. Although it is not impossible, it is much more difficult to prove ill motives of the heart's intention than it is to prove an outward breach of a behavioral code. For example, if it was witnessed that one broke into a car not his own, hotwired it and drove it off, it would then be considered a clear cut case of breaking the law. But to prove what an individual had at heart when he committed an act is not such a clear cut or obvious action we can point to and see outwardly. That is because intent is an invisible or spirit motive of the inner or spiritual nature of man, and not an outward act that all may see. Yes, ill motives will result in evil acts. However, one's actions, even if they may injure another party, are not proof positive of one having an evil motive.

Likewise, manslaughter and murder are both a crime. In both cases one is held responsible for taking the life of another. However, murder is punished much more severely than manslaughter. The difference between the two is, again, the intent. One would be found guilty of manslaughter because he took the life of another through some sort of gross negligence, like having an automobile accident while driving intoxicated resulting in loss of life. Whereas to be found guilty of murder, it must be established there was a willful intent or motive to take the life of another. With manslaughter, criminal negligence needs to be proven, but with an absence of intent or motive to take a life. For it to be murder, there is an intent and motive to take a life and that motive or intent must be proven. Even the laws of the United States have a spiritual (invisible) aspect to them.

Note: Wisdom, perception, inspiration, intent, motivation, and feelings are some of the attributes of man's spirit.

So when it says to love the Lord your God with all your heart and with all your soul and with all your mind and with all your strength, our spiritual intent and our motives must be purely and unselfishly doing so out of love for God and not for what we get out of God. Just like when it comes to murder and fraud, the invisible or spiritual intent is the most important aspect of our worship towards God.

The last commandment is to not covet. If one covets it may result in evil outward acts, however, it is by nature an inward heart posture, a perception, and motive. To covet is not an outward act. To covet is to behold things with a sense of entitlement and jealousy—to want what has not been given by God. Therefore, just as the first, this final commandment is a spiritual boundary speaking to our inward invisible natures, and is not an outward moral behavioral code.

Having the first and last commandments spiritual in nature as they are, every commandment sandwiched between them cannot be broken without first transgressing these two commandments by the spirit and mind of the man. You have to break the beginning and ending commandments in your heart before you can even have a mind to break any of the commandments in between them in a behavioral way.

This makes it true when it says that if you stumble on even one commandment you are guilty of breaking them all (Jas 2:10). And also that: we know the law is spiritual, but I am unspiritual (Ro 7:14). Meaning, Paul might be able to keep the outward behavioral codes (in his estimation), but he is unable to keep the spiritual aspect of the very same laws. Thus, he is unspiritual in the face of adhering to the perfect laws of God, which are first and foremost spiritual, even before they are outward behavioral codes.

We have an unspiritual understanding that assumes that if we do not transgress the behavioral aspect of the law, we are keeping the laws and not breaking them. Likewise, the law that was meant to serve God's will and to respect and honor other people, we use to justify the evil we do. We are forever looking for ways of committing evil and self-interest acts while technically being within the boundaries of what the behavioral aspect of the law allows. We use the laws to serve ourselves, not God, or our fellow man. This, Paul tells us in Romans, is breaking the spirit of the law. For the purpose of the law was never meant to justify selfishly serving self, but to live in harmony and fairness with those around us, and to serve God.

As such we (man) believe for the most part that it doesn't matter where we let our feelings, desires, and thoughts go as long as we don't outwardly break the laws in a behavioral sense. And therefore, what we do or don't do is the only thing that counts. The truth is, this is not only a superficially shortsighted misconception (unspiritual), but it is false to the truth, and is eternally deadly. Jesus spoke to the Jewish religious leaders of His day of this same matter:

NIV Mt 23:13 "*Woe to you, teachers of the law and Pharisees, you hypocrites! You shut the kingdom of heaven in men's faces. You yourselves do not enter, nor will you let those enter who are trying to.*

Jesus says, "you shut the Kingdom of Heaven in men's faces." And "You yourselves do not enter in." He is referring to the fact that they do not keep the spiritual aspect or the righteous requirements of the law, and as such, they are not reconciled with God, and will not become celestial humans living in the New Jerusalem ruling over natural humans as a part of His 1,000 year Kingdom here on earth. In addition, they teach their converts the same superficial or behavioral observance of the law so they too can use it to serve themselves instead of God. They convert people to be right with God, however, after doing so they don't just stop at not teaching them how to conform to God through the law, but actually teach them how to selfishly use the law in a way that actually disqualifies them from being reconciled with God or becoming a celestial human and part of His Kingdom to come. It is no small wonder why Jesus calls them hypocrites. No other word could describe them more precisely.

Note: It is important to realize that every time Jesus talked about the Kingdom of Heaven or the Kingdom of God He is talking about the supernatural cohabitating with the natural world. This is something that His prophets spoke would happen. He will bring the whole world under His submission, reign 1,000 years, then after the last day of the natural earth and its universe, He will continue to reign for eternity in the spiritual realm. The earth and the natural universe, however, will be thrown into the lake of fire and be no more at that time. All the people of the earth will be resurrected, judged and it will be determined who will also (at that time) become celestial humans, adding to the numbers of who already have become so, and live on for eternity in the celestial city, in the spirit realm. Jesus does not want to come down to earth with only the New Jerusalem, His Father, and His army angels. He wants celestial humans to be a part of His court when He rules the natural humans of the earth for 1,000 years. This is why He has come before He brings the whole world into submission to Himself. He desires to take/recruit for Himself people to be celestial humans to rule with Him when He comes for the purpose of establishing His Kingdom.

In addition, this means there are two chances to make the cut and become a celestial human. Now and up to the end of the great tribulation, and then 1,000 years later on the last day. The requirements on the last day are decidedly less to qualify. It is then that your deeds can earn you a place in eternity. However, to become a part of it now is not by deeds, but by receiving His Holy Spirit and becoming in union with Jesus as one whole person. He died to His body, you die to your life in your body and His disembodied Spirit has expression through your body and life in the body. This is why Jesus is quoted as having said to those who did works in His Name to further His cause, "get away from me you evil doers, I never knew you." At face value this might seem unfair if you devote your whole life to be a pastor and build churches for Him. The truth is that doing so might get you into eternity on the last day when you will be judged by how you conducted yourself as a human, even how you treated other humans, especially those who were in union with Jesus. However, this means nothing when it comes to being included in His Kingdom of Heaven here on earth. To be a part of that, there is a whole different criteria.

Jesus said to the others, "I never knew you . . ." This seems strange for God to say when He knows every single being and knows all things. What He meant was He didn't "know them" in the Biblical sense. He wasn't one-flesh with them. He was not in spiritual union or marriage with them. Which, sadly for them who labored in vain, is the qualification to be included in His Kingdom of Heaven. For the record, those not found in spiritual union with Him, although Christians when it comes time for the great tribulation, will not be raptured with those who will be. However, if they endure the great tribulation without taking the mark of the beast, or worshiping the antichrist, or coming off their testimony of Jesus even to death, they will receive a celestial body and most certainly be celestial humans in His court during His 1,000 year reign. According to the book of Revelation this will be called the "first resurrection."

This situation is why He repeated over and over to the Jews, in the Gospels, who were meant to be the celestial humans with Him during His 1,000 year reign, that the "first shall be last and the last shall be first." Meaning, although they were already His people first and were meant to be by His side as celestial humans during His Kingdom, they will have to wait it out, disembodied in Hades, after they die a natural death until the last day and the resurrection of the dead to be judged. This is because of their rejection of Him. Instead of being the first and part of His Kingdom rule over the earth, they will be last. It is then that they may qualify and finally become celestial humans, living on with Him for eternity in heaven/the spirit realm.

Conversely, those people, even the gentiles and sinners (the last), who do follow Him, will fill up His court and be celestial humans with Him during His 1,000 year reign (the first shall be last to enter into eternity and the last will do so first). This situation is also the meaning behind several of His parables. Like, for example, the wedding when nobody who was invited would come, and the master instead sent his laborers out to the streets to fill up his house with others instead of those who were invited. Below, Jesus shares with them (the first) what disqualifies them from being the first. Which is how they are careful to follow the behavioral aspects of the Law, however, the spiritual aspect they all but ignore and still believe they are righteous.

NAS MT 23:14 *"Woe to you, scribes and Pharisees, hypocrites, because you devour widows' houses, and for a pretense you make long prayers; therefore you will receive greater condemnation.*
NLT Mt 23:15 *Yes, how terrible it will be for you teachers of religious law and you Pharisees. For you cross land and sea to make one convert, and then you turn him into twice the son of hell as you yourselves are.*
NLT Mt 23:16 *"Blind guides! How terrible it will be for you! For you say that it means nothing to swear 'by God's Temple'—you can break that oath. But then you say that it is binding to swear 'by the gold in the Temple.'*

NLT Mt 23:17 *Blind fools! Which is greater, the gold, or the Temple that makes the gold sacred?*

NLT Mt 23:18 *And you say that to take an oath 'by the altar' can be broken, but to swear 'by the gifts on the altar' is binding!*

NLT Mt 23:19 *How blind! For which is greater, the gift on the altar, or the altar that makes the gift sacred?*

NLT Mt 23:20 *When you swear 'by the altar,' you are swearing by it and by everything on it.*

NLT Mt 23:21 *And when you swear 'by the Temple,' you are swearing by it and by God, who lives in it.*

NLT Mt 23:22 *And when you swear 'by heaven,' you are swearing by the throne of God and by God, who sits on the throne.*

In thinking this way, making keeping their word a matter of "technicalities" so that they can justify not keeping their word (in a legalistic way), is what led to a childhood way of doing the same. Many will remember in your youth when you learned about crossing your fingers. If you held your hands out of sight and crossed your fingers or crossed your legs then when you broke your promise or did not keep your word, all you would say was, "I had my fingers crossed so what I said doesn't count!" Or you could promise never intending to keep your word, and then all you had to do was to cross your fingers and you could tell people what they wanted to hear and later claim, "it doesn't count!" In addition, if you want to give yourself any kind of credibility you would start or end your sentence with the phrase, "I swear to God . . ."

This is brought up because it is rather incredible how many things we learn to do as children that seem harmless but are completely in line with everything that makes us unable to behold God and the spiritual in a proper light. Think about this occasion and the seemingly innocent nursery rhymes we learn as children which are about death and violence.

NLT Mt 23:23 *"How terrible it will be for you teachers of religious law and you Pharisees. Hypocrites! For you are careful to tithe even the tiniest part of your income, but you ignore the important things of the law—justice, mercy, and faith. You should tithe, yes, but you should not leave undone the more important things.*

NLT Mt 23:24 *Blind guides! You strain your water so you won't accidentally swallow a gnat; then you swallow a camel!*

NLT Mt 23:25 *"How terrible it will be for you teachers of religious law and you Pharisees. Hypocrites! You are so careful to clean the outside of the cup and the dish, but inside you are filthy—full of greed and self-indulgence!*

NLT Mt 23:26 *Blind Pharisees! First wash the inside of the cup, and then the outside will become clean, too.*

NLT Mt 23:27 *"How terrible it will be for you teachers of religious law and you Pharisees. Hypocrites! You are like whitewashed tombs—beautiful on the outside but filled on the inside with dead people's bones and all sorts of impurity.*

NLT Mt 23:28 *You try to look like upright people outwardly, but inside your hearts are filled with hypocrisy and lawlessness.*

CHAPTER 2

The Two Lies

In actuality, both of these commandments (the first and the last) are in answer to the two lies Adam ingested when he ate of the fruit of the knowledge of good and evil, corrupting the human spirit and unrepairibly skewing it's world view forever.

The two lies:

1) The first lie is that there is something outside their garden which will make them truly happy, or that the grass is greener on the other side of the hill. The serpent (inspired by the Devil) caused Adam and Eve to believe there was something good and desirous outside of what God had given them. It gave them a sense that God was cheating them from something, causing them to doubt God and His intentions and trust the Devil more than God. This is the root of covetousness, which the last law addresses.

The whole thing is more than a lie but a double lie, or a lie on two levels. The obvious lie is that it was erroneous judgment on their part to believe God was short changing them out of something, or holding something back, and that they should trust someone more than God. The reality was that the Devil tricked them into taking on his spirit of rebellion towards God, wanting something outside of what God gave (to covet).

However, the double lie is that we think it is an overwhelming desire within us that we can't help which makes us want, for example, the neighbor's wife (the object of our desire). But the lie is that it is the spirit of the Devil inside us that Adam and Eve ingested into their beings (the human spirit), which gives us the feeling that we have to have what is not ours.

The true nature of the spirit within us is that it is not a desire to have the woman stirring within the man to the point he can't help himself. It is instead the veiled desire of the Devil stirring within. The veil is to believe what stirs the soul is desire for the woman. The true essence of the desire of the Devil is a rebellious, defiant, and a vicious determination in the spirit of the Devil that wants independence from God. This is what resides in man because of what Adam and Eve ingested and what makes man want that which God has not given to him.

As a result (and at the cost of everything), that compelling desire is to want whatever God has not offered, what is taboo, and then to reject what God has given. This is the truth of what drives a man to throw away his wife, children and, most importantly, his standing with God to have the neighbor's wife. This explains why when so many people finally get what they think they want, they realize it really was not what they were looking for. This is because they were deceived. When the man finally gets what he wants, all it satisfies is the covetous spirit essence within the man's sin-nature which wants to break free from God and have what was not given him by God.

In sum, the woman was merely a vehicle, the veiled desires masking the covetous spirit within that had expression and was satisfied. Naturally and as a result, once that is satisfied and its desire has been accomplished (corrupting and destroying the relationship between God and man), there is not much, if any, spirit desire left inside the man inspiring and compelling him to continue wanting what he traded all that was good for. He did not know what he had until he lost it. This means it was not really him who wanted it, but the covetous spirit of the Devil within who did it for ulterior reasons and was satisfied.

NIV Ro 7:20 Now if I do what I do not want to do, it is no longer I who do it, but it is sin living in me that does it.

NIV Ro 7:21 So I find this law at work: When I want to do good, evil is right there with me.

Man truly does not understand the spirit forces and motives which stir his heart.

Amnon and Tamar

NIV 2Sa 13:1 In the course of time, Amnon son of David fell in love with Tamar, the beautiful sister of Absalom son of David.

NIV 2Sa 13:2 Amnon became frustrated to the point of illness on account of his sister Tamar, for she was a virgin, and it seemed impossible for him to do anything to her.

NIV 2Sa 13:3 Now Amnon had a friend named Jonadab son of Shimeah, David's brother. Jonadab was a very shrewd man.

NIV 2Sa 13:4 He asked Amnon, "Why do you, the king's son, look so haggard morning after morning? Won't you tell me?" Amnon said to him, "I'm in love with Tamar, my brother Absalom's sister."

NIV 2Sa 13:5 "Go to bed and pretend to be ill," Jonadab said. "When your father comes to see you, say to him, 'I would like my sister Tamar to come and give me something to eat. Let her prepare the food in my sight so I may watch her and then eat it from her hand.' "

NIV 2Sa 13:6 So Amnon lay down and pretended to be ill. When the king came to see him, Amnon said to him, "I would like my sister Tamar to come and make some special bread in my sight, so I may eat from her hand."

NIV 2Sa 13:7 David sent word to Tamar at the palace: "Go to the house of your brother Amnon and prepare some food for him."

NIV 2Sa 13:8 So Tamar went to the house of her brother Amnon, who was lying down. She took some dough, kneaded it, made the bread in his sight and baked it.

NIV 2Sa 13:9 *Then she took the pan and served him the bread, but he refused to eat. "Send everyone out of here," Amnon said. So everyone left him.*

NIV 2Sa 13:10 *Then Amnon said to Tamar, "Bring the food here into my bedroom so I may eat from your hand." And Tamar took the bread she had prepared and brought it to her brother Amnon in his bedroom.*

NIV 2Sa 13:11 *But when she took it to him to eat, he grabbed her and said, "Come to bed with me, my sister."*

NIV 2Sa 13:12 *"Don't, my brother!" she said to him. "Don't force me. Such a thing should not be done in Israel! Don't do this wicked thing.*

NIV 2Sa 13:13 *What about me? Where could I get rid of my disgrace? And what about you? You would be like one of the wicked fools in Israel. Please speak to the king; he will not keep me from being married to you."*

NIV 2Sa 13:14 *But he refused to listen to her, and since he was stronger than she, he raped her.*

NIV 2Sa 13:15 *Then Amnon hated her with intense hatred. In fact, he hated her more than he had loved her. Amnon said to her, "Get up and get out!"*

NIV 2Sa 13:16 *"No!" she said to him. "Sending me away would be a greater wrong than what you have already done to me." But he refused to listen to her.*

NIV 2Sa 13:17 *He called his personal servant and said, "Get this woman out of here and bolt the door after her."*

Again, the man is deceived. It was not a desire of love for the woman overpowering him, but a rebellious spirit motive which had been infused into the human spirit within his very essence taking advantage of his wandering eyes. The true and unveiled objective of the desire the man feels is the sinful spirit within which is inflamed with a desire to reject God, what He has given, and finally to be independent of Him, having something outside of Him. This lie, this spirit of rebellion against God, this desire to have something outside of our garden is called, "covetousness."

2) The allure, which finally convinced Adam and Eve to partake of the fruit of the knowledge of both good and evil, was that they could ingest something that would make them like God, or a god. That something the Bible calls, "wisdom." It reads that the fruit was "desirable for gaining wisdom" (Gen 3:6). Ezekiel tells us about this very wisdom of the Devil which Adam and Eve saw as desirable:

NIV Eze 28:17 *Your heart became proud on account of your beauty, and you corrupted your wisdom because of your splendor.*

Wisdom, in a Biblical context, can be defined as a set of values by which to perceive through. Wisdom is an attribute of man's spirit and, as such, functions from a place beyond words, or, before words enter into the mix. The intellect is a function of the soul or mind of the man. It is here that man assigns words to describe his spirit feelings and perceptions so he may think about them. However, before words are used to describe and reason with, wisdom dictates a point of perspective, a world view, which produces the feelings, attitudes, and outlook by which man begins to perceive and understand things through.

Wisdom is beyond words. No matter how intelligent and sharp at reasoning a mind might be, it is the spirit wisdom of the man which filters through its framework (values) all that the man may sense. Then, his mind might try to find understanding by using word descriptions of what he senses spiritually. One can be highly intelligent, even possessing near perfect language skills, but be unwise, possessing a very shallow insight into matters. Likewise, one can be very wise, having an extremely insightful perception of matters with an ability to conceptualize the deepest things, but not have his intelligence and word knowledge very developed.

The serpent promised Adam and Eve a wisdom which would make them like God.

NIV Ge 3:5 *"For God knows that when you eat of it your eyes will be opened, and you will be like God, knowing good and evil."*

The lie is that, in doing so, they merely took on a spirit wisdom, a false perception, or false world view that sees and perceives all things as if they were God. Their world view sees things from a perspective that makes them the beginning and end of all things, the center of all things, with everything revolving around them and their purposes, as being self-sustaining, self-gratifying, and painfully self-conscious, seeing things in light of how all things affect them and make them feel, and so on.

If you were to ask the average person if he thinks he is God, he would say, "heavens no!" However, the same person perceives his world and responds to life as if he is. The lie is that the seemingly desirable wisdom Adam and Eve ingested did nothing towards making them God. It only caused them to falsely view and respond to their world in light of a fantastic delusion—that they were.

Two Kinds of Wisdom

NIV Jas 3:13 *Who is wise and understanding among you? Let him show it by his good life, by deeds done in the humility that comes from wisdom.*

NIV Jas 3:14 *But if you harbor bitter envy and selfish ambition in your hearts, do not boast about it or deny the truth.*

NIV Jas 3:15 *Such "wisdom" does not come down from heaven but is earthly, unspiritual, of the devil.*

NIV Jas 3:16 *For where you have envy and selfish ambition, there you find disorder and every evil practice.*

NIV Jas 3:17 *But the wisdom that comes from heaven is first of all pure; then peace-loving, considerate, submissive, full of mercy and good fruit, impartial and sincere.*

NIV Jas 3:18 *Peacemakers who sow in peace raise a harvest of righteousness.*

Note: Although James tells us that there are two kinds of wisdom, the second kind (the one which comes down from heaven), is the wisdom of the Spirit of Jesus Christ. It was not available to humans from the time of Adam until Jesus released His disembodied Spirit in the earth to humanity through His death. And then, only to those who receive (take into their heart) and operate out of His Spirit power and wisdom. In other words, to the partakers of the New Covenant. Prior to the New Covenant promises, the Old Covenant gave as its way to reconcile with God the perfect law (the ten commandments).

All the children of Adam and Eve, the human race, have within their spirit essence this life-principle (the spirit of the Devil), which includes the Devil's wisdom and its values, as a part of their human spirit. This, thereby, dooms them to spiritually sin against the True God while having a very superficial or shallow perception (unspiritual) of life. James admonishes us to not take pride in this kind of insight even if it helps us get ahead in the world. The first commandment addresses this lie and corrects the world view of the (true) follower of it. Jesus says:

Mt 6:24 *"No one can serve two masters. Either he will hate the one and love the other, or he will be devoted to the one and despise the other. . .*

Jesus also makes us aware in Revelation that when we decide matters in light of how they serve us, we have lost our first love. Our first, or preferential love is ourselves and no longer God at that point. So then, if we follow the first commandment and love and serve God with the whole of our being in preference to Him even before ourselves, we have successfully made God our first love and have successfully corrected our wisdom values so that we perceive things in a way that are not in defiance to God or false to the truth. We no longer see things in a light which makes us God through the perception of our wisdom.

Note: To be unspiritual, or superficial does not necessarily mean that you are unaware of spiritual matters. Although in most cases that is exactly the case. However, you can be very aware and concerned about the spiritual, but conceive and understand the spiritual in terms of outward behavioral matters only, or as behavioral issues and concepts.

Amp 1Co 2:13 *And we are setting these truths forth in words not taught by human wisdom but taught by the [Holy] Spirit, combining and interpreting spiritual truths with spiritual language [to those who possess the Holy Spirit].*

Amp 1Co 2:14 *But the natural, nonspiritual man does not accept or welcome or admit into his heart the gifts and teachings and revelations of the Spirit of God, for they are folly (meaningless nonsense) to him; and he is incapable of knowing them [of progressively recognizing, understanding, and becoming better acquainted with them] because they are spiritually discerned and estimated and appreciated.*

NIV Ro 7:14 *We know that the law is spiritual; but I am unspiritual, sold as a slave to sin.*

NIV Ro 7:15 *I do not understand what I do. For what I want to do I do not do, but what I hate I do.*

NIV Ro 7:16 *And if I do what I do not want to do, I agree that the law is good.*

NIV Ro 7:17 *As it is, it is no longer I myself who do it, but it is sin living in me.*

NIV Ro 7:18 *I know that nothing good lives in me, that is, in my sinful nature. For I have the desire to do what is good, but I cannot carry it out.*

NIV Ro 7:19 *For what I do is not the good I want to do; no, the evil I do not want to do—this I keep on doing.*

NIV Ro 7:20 *Now if I do what I do not want to do, it is no longer I who do it, but it is sin living in me that does it.*

NIV Ro 7:21 *So I find this law at work: When I want to do good, evil is right there with me.*

NIV Ro 7:22 *For in my inner being I delight in God's law;*

NIV Ro 7:23 *but I see another law at work in the members of my body, waging war against the law of my mind and making me a prisoner of the law of sin at work within my members.*

NIV Ro 7:24 *What a wretched man I am! Who will rescue me from this body of death?*

NIV Ro 7:25 *Thanks be to God—through Jesus Christ our Lord! So then, I myself in my mind am a slave to God's law, but in the sinful nature a slave to the law of sin.*

These laws, as it turns out, are genius! They are perfect! They are a gift to the children of the promise! They are not just moral behavioral codes to live within, no! If we keep them, even not knowing the damage the fruit of the knowledge of good and evil did within the human spirit, it will still perfect us causing us to be like Adam before the fall. Yes, Paul is right, the law is spiritual and its purpose reaches far beyond external behavior and how we treat each other.

If anyone were able to both spiritually and outwardly follow these commandments handed down to us from God through Moses, he would be in right standing with God. He would then possess a corrected world view that would make keeping the commandments natural, as well as, causing his perception/world view to be in compliance and in union with the Spirit behind the law, and void of covetousness. Our hearts would literally perceive, understand, and be moved by the Spirit of God, and thus we would be in total conformity to Him—inside and out. Within the laws of God there is a secret passage that the human heart can pass through to be right with God.

The two lies ingested at the garden are overcome by those who keep this perfect law and its spiritual aspect! However, there is a defect in man which prevents him from spiritually conforming to the perfect law Moses gave and thereby being reconciled with God. The law was not given to harm, but to perfect; it was a gift so that the human heart would know how to right himself and therefore be reconciled with God. No one in humanity has ever been able to overcome this defect and truly be reconciled to God. We have been hopelessly lost.

CHAPTER 3

The Defect

There is a defect in us that the Lord experientially revealed by giving us His laws. This defect is as described in the previous chapter; we are unspiritual in our perception (wisdom), and in being so (as James says), we are false to the truth and are in defiance to God (Amp Jas 3:14). Hebrews explains:

Amp Heb 8:6 *But as it now is, He [Christ] has acquired a [priestly] ministry which is as much superior and more excellent [than the old] as the covenant (the agreement) of which He is the Mediator (the Arbiter, Agent) is superior and more excellent, [because] it is enacted and rests upon more important (sublimer, higher, and nobler) promises.*

Amp Heb 8:7 *For if that first covenant had been without* *defect,* *there would have been no room for another one or an attempt to institute another one.*

Amp Heb 8:8 *However, He finds fault with them [showing its inadequacy] when He says, Behold, the days will come, says the Lord, when I will make and ratify a new covenant or agreement with the house of Israel and with the house of Judah.*

Amp Heb 8:9 *It will not be like the covenant that I made with their forefathers on the day when I grasped them by the hand to help and relieve them and to lead them out from the land of Egypt, for they did not abide in My agreement with them, and so I withdrew My favor and disregarded them, says the Lord.*

Amp Heb 8:10 *For this is the covenant that I will make with the house of Israel after those days, says the Lord: I will imprint My laws upon their minds, even upon their innermost thoughts and understanding, and engrave them upon their hearts; and I will be their God, and they shall be My people.*

Amp Heb 8:11 *And it will nevermore be necessary for each one to teach his neighbor and his fellow citizen or each one his brother, saying, Know (perceive, have knowledge of, and get acquainted by experience with) the Lord, for all will know Me, from the smallest to the greatest of them.*

Amp Heb 8:12 *For I will be merciful and gracious toward their sins and I will remember their deeds of unrighteousness no more.*

Amp Heb 8:13 *When God speaks of a new [covenant or agreement], He makes the first one obsolete (out of use). And what is obsolete (out of use and annulled because of age) is ripe for disappearance and to be dispensed with altogether.*

This is a very important matter outlined above. If the perfect law handed down through Moses is proven inadequate to save and reconcile man spiritually to God because of a defect (in man) so great that it causes God to establish a New Covenant while annulling the first, then it makes this "defect" an urgently profound matter. It is the central and core issue which prevents man from reconciling with God. As a result of the perfect law of God, this defect is exposed as a total inability on man's part to first conform, and finally reconcile with God spiritually (in his essence—in his invisible nature).

It is obviously important to have a clarity about this defect. However, we don't know what we don't know, making it hard to relate to all that surrounds our defect. In turn, it stands to reason that we can be oblivious to its significance. The defect of having a wisdom which is unspiritual and from the Devil makes it impossible for man to comply with the spiritual aspects of the law given to us. Or as Paul calls it, "the righteous requirements of the law" (Ro 8:4). This in turn makes it impossible to reconcile with God, especially since God is Spirit. Again, Paul spoke (above) about how this defect affects us: The wisdom of God's Spirit is folly (meaningless nonsense), and we are incapable of knowing the true wisdom of God because it is spiritually discerned and estimated and appreciated.

Regarding its significance, Hebrews tells us this defect is the sole factor that makes the Old Covenant obsolete and annulled, causing the need for a New Covenant. Likewise, the New Covenant is designed and put into effect with the express purpose to address and overcome the defect which prevents man from conforming to God in a spiritual sense, and then, as a result, reconciling with Him. This New Covenant accomplishes what the Old Covenant could not. It was so urgent and necessary in God's heart that God Himself came in the body and suffered all that He did to make a way for man to overcome this defect.

Jesus came to give man a gift which would give him the wisdom and power to master the defect of being unspiritual and too weak to overcome. You could call this gift, the gift of salvation. This being the case, it should be the main objective of the Christ follower to make his focus exploring and learning to operate in the gift of a new and heavenly wisdom Jesus gave at the cost of His life. To not do so would be to deny the power and gift He gave at the expense of His life. It would render His death useless, profaning all He accomplished. To not apply its power towards the defect, makes the New Covenant as impotent as the Old in restoring man to God. As such, let us take a closer look at this most important factor the Christ follower has inhibiting his relationship with God (the defect).

The Lord is not a liar or a breaker of promises

My father used to say while driving down the road and because of our discord, "If I have to pull this car over and come into the back seat, then some heads are going to roll." As it turns out, this defect is so profoundly debilitating that it requires God Himself to come here from out of the realm of the spirit, be born, and then die but remain in the world with His disembodied Spirit. To do so is to be outside of His true nature and natural habitat.

God is Spirit; He lives in the spirit realm which is comprised of spiritual matter just as the body of God is comprised of spiritual matter. He is a spiritual being, not a natural being. A natural man has a body made up of natural matter (the elements of the physical universe) and he lives in the natural realm. In order to save us, God chose to change His solely spiritual nature (embodiment) to also have a physical nature (embodiment), just as a human being. He did this that we could take on His original nature and become spiritual or celestial humans. In doing so, we would escape the doom the physical universe, including all natural matter, is sentenced with. The physical will be done away with forever, but the spiritual will remain for eternity. He did all of this so that we might choose to become in spiritual union with His Spirit—ingesting and adapting to His Spirit just as Adam and Eve did with the spirit of the Devil. This Spirit, however, would provide us the ability and power to overcome our defect.

NIV Ge 15:9 *So the LORD said to him, "Bring me a heifer, a goat and a ram, each three years old, along with a dove and a young pigeon."*

NIV Ge 15:10 *Abram brought all these to him, cut them in two and arranged the halves opposite each other; the birds, however, he did not cut in half.*

NIV Ge 15:11 *Then birds of prey came down on the carcasses, but Abram drove them away.*

NIV Ge 15:12 *As the sun was setting, Abram fell into a deep sleep, and a thick and dreadful darkness came over him.*

NIV Ge 15:13 *Then the LORD said to him, "Know for certain that your descendants will be strangers in a country not their own, and they will be enslaved and mistreated four hundred years.*

NIV Ge 15:14 *But I will punish the nation they serve as slaves, and afterward they will come out with great possessions.*

NIV Ge 15:15 *You, however, will go to your fathers in peace and be buried at a good old age.*

NIV Ge 15:16 *In the fourth generation your descendants will come back here, for the sin of the Amorites has not yet reached its full measure."*

NIV Ge 15:17 When the sun had set and darkness had fallen, a smoking firepot with a blazing torch appeared and passed between the pieces.
NIV Ge 15:18 On that day the LORD made a covenant with Abram

It may seem strange to do what is described above, even horrifying. However, Abram (Abraham) understood the significance. This type of oath was practiced during his time. It was a blood oath, and it was the ultimate oath which no one would make frivolously. When making this oath to keep a promise, one would cut the animals in two, long ways, and lay the halves opposite each other in a line, forming a path of blood between the two sides of the animals. Then the one making the oath would walk up and down in the blood between the halves while declaring out loud his promises, ending with, "may what happened to these animals happen to me if I do not keep my promises." The Lord made an oath concerning His promises to Abraham, and He was represented by the smoking firepot and blazing torch passing between the sacrificed animal halves. It is said that the life (spirit) is in the blood which was spilled out on the ground by these sacrificed animals.

There is no reconciliation between God and man without spiritual conformity to His will on man's part.

NIV Ge 4:5 ... So Cain was very angry, and his face was downcast (dejected).
NIV Ge 4:6 Then the LORD said to Cain, "Why are you angry? Why is your face downcast (dejected)?
NIV Ge 4:7 If you do what is right, will you not be accepted? But if you do not do what is right, sin is crouching at your door; it desires to have you, but you must master it.

The Lord's oath recorded in the Bible helps us understand how serious this defect of ours is, and how nothing on earth or within the power of man can overcome it. In the history of mankind since its second generation (taught to us by Cain's noncompliance), man has not been able to do this simple task: To simply do what is right by God and therefore be accepted and in harmony with Him. Instead, sin, ever ready to pounce, got the best of Cain and has been besting every single man born of a woman ever since. We truly do have a defect that prevents us from being right with God no matter how hard we try.

In order to keep His promises that were otherwise proven to be unkeepable, the Lord had to submit to the consequences of His blood oath to make a way for His promises to be kept. Through His volunteer submission of the punishment of being beaten and whipped, and through His death on the cross as a sacrificial lamb, and by the spilling out of His life, His blood on the ground, He fulfilled the consequences of His oath that had gone unfulfilled.

In doing so, He took the measures that created a New Covenant with new promises which were indeed finally enough to overcome the defect in man (which had formerly caused His promises to go unfulfilled). All this was necessary because of our inability to respond to His life giving laws in a spiritually conforming way.

When I was young my memory was such that if I went through the trouble to write something down so I would not forget, I would not need the list I wrote. If I went through the trouble to write it, the act of writing was enough that I would remember everything I wrote. I would write the list and just leave it at home. It was the same with names and phone numbers. I had unused lists, names and phone numbers laying all around my house, left wherever I wrote them. To me this was a weird conundrum which I let bother me. I reasoned, "what is the use of going through the trouble of writing it down when I did not need the list?" However, if I did not write it down I would forget. As a young boy I would let this perplex me and I thought about it often.

The Lord made an oath which could not be performed on account of the ones He was trying to help. However, by suffering the consequences for not being able to fully fulfill the promises, He made a way to fulfill the promises. Similarly the question is the same; if there was a way, why should He have to suffer the consequences of there not being a way?

Praise God I had my conundrum (as bothersome as it was), and I did not have His.

When the Lord made that oath, He already knew the promises He had made were unkeepable because of man's defect. It was no secret to God that man would show himself unworthy of the promises that God had offered, and instead only worthy of destruction, just as before the flood when it was said about man:

NIV Ge 6:5 The LORD saw how great man's wickedness on the earth had become, and that every inclination of the thoughts of his heart was only evil all the time.

NIV Ge 6:6 The LORD was grieved that he had made man on the earth, and his heart was filled with pain.

NIV Ge 6:7 So the LORD said, "I will wipe mankind, whom I have created, from the face of the earth—men and animals, and creatures that move along the ground, and birds of the air—for I am grieved that I have made them."

When I was young I asked the nuns during Catechism class if God could do anything. In confidence and without hesitation they would respond with a resounding, "Yes! He could—He is God!" I would then ask a second question. "If that is true, can He make a rock so big that even He could not pick it up?" That, again, would earn me a prompt and personal consultation with our priest (the principal).

God purposefully put Himself in a no win situation. It has to be asked, "Why do this?" Man was responsible for his own defiance towards God, and, as such, made himself fit only for being destroyed.

Amp Mt 23:37 *How often would I have gathered your children together as a mother* (hen) *fowl gathers her brood* (of chicks) *under her wings, and you refused!*

God is innocent in the matter; however, the children of the promise refused to let God bless them. Because of the defect, they unwittingly rejected God's blessings. The Lord then took responsibility in accordance to the oath because He could not bless them.

The children of the promise:

The Lord had done everything to prepare the hearts of His people so they could follow His perfect law and thereby bring conformity resulting in reconciliation. He remembered the problem with Cain and how he served himself instead of God which resulted in worse sins, starting with murder, even after being warned.

In answer to that, before He gave His perfect law, He wanted to give them every chance to succeed, as painful as it would be. When their numbers were enough, He oppressed the children of the promise with forced servitude for 400 years. Through the bondage of slavery, they learned to serve the will of someone other than their own. Likewise, they learned to live for someone other than themselves—their lives were literally not their own. They lived to serve the pleasure of someone else besides themselves. All of this was to prepare their hearts to simply have the capacity to joyfully serve not their own, but the will of God who, unlike Egypt, would bless them in every way for doing so.

It was only then, with this newly formed heart that forced servitude had shaped and molded, that the Lord took them by the hand and led them out of bondage, and gave them His perfect law. Which, if followed, holistically would cause them to conform to God's will and thereby be reconciled and blessed as He promised Abraham. However, the result was that their defect still got in the way and He had to turn His face away from them. He deservedly turned them over to the curses of not keeping the law, while letting His promises of blessings go unfulfilled. He did this when He gave them over to Babylon for 70 years. Again, something He already knew would happen.

What was the point then? Why did I have to write things down if I didn't need the list? Why couldn't I remember without writing? Why did the Lord of all have to suffer the consequences of not being able to fulfill His promises? When after all, suffering the consequences made a way so He could fulfill His promises, thereby making the consequences unnecessary? And finally, why did the Lord put the children of the promise through 400 years of oppressive bondage and 40 years in the desert knowing in the end their defect would prevent Him from carrying out His promises and He would have to do something different (a New Covenant) to qualify them?

Paul answered all but my conundrum:

NIV Ro 7:7 What shall we say, then? Is the law sin? Certainly not! Indeed I would not have known what sin was except through the law. For I would not have known what coveting really was if the law had not said, "Do not covet."
NIV Ro 7:8 But sin, seizing the opportunity afforded by the commandment, produced in me every kind of covetous desire. For apart from law, sin is dead.
NIV Ro 7:9 Once I was alive apart from law; but when the commandment came, sin sprang to life and I died.
NIV Ro 7:10 I found that the very commandment that was intended to bring life actually brought death.
NIV Ro 7:11 For sin, seizing the opportunity afforded by the commandment, deceived me, and through the commandment put me to death.
NIV Ro 7:12 So then, the law is holy, and the commandment is holy, righteous and good.
NIV Ro 7:13 Did that which is good, then, become death to me? By no means! But in order that sin might be recognized as sin, it produced death in me through what

was good, so that through the commandment sin might become (recognized as) utterly sinful.

The spiritual condition of those who are unspiritual and are oblivious to the spiritual aspect of conforming to the Lord is recognized through the law! The law revealed to man something he could not see about himself, something God tried to point out to Cain. Giving the law was a necessary step in the long term plan of God's so that He could save man from destruction. Through failure of keeping the law and its spiritual aspect, man can finally recognize his own defect which is stopping him from reconciling with his Maker. In this way, when the New Covenant came man could know what it was meant to overcome and thereby take advantage of and function in the New Covenant power which would help him defeat his defect.

The New Covenant does for us what the Old Covenant could not overcome in Cain. That is, the spirit of sin within, crouching at the door, seizing every opportunity (as Paul noted) causing us to be impotent, rendering us unable to master the spirit of sin within. Just as Cain had failed to do. That is the defect: Neither we nor Cain could master sin (the spirit of sin in our human spirit) as God admonished was necessary, and therefore instead do what is right by God causing us to be accepted by Him. God gave us the Law as an aide to master sin, however, all it accomplished was exposing the defect preventing us from doing so. Every step in God's long term plan of salvation of man is a necessary step to make the impossible, possible!

Regarding my conundrum; as things are now, not only can I no longer remember what I wrote on the list, but I can't remember where I left the list, making the whole thing a moot point.

The patience and kindness of the Lord:

NIV Ps 145:8 *The LORD is gracious and compassionate, slow to anger and rich in love.*
NIV Ps 145:9 *The LORD is good to all; he has compassion on all he has made.*
NIV Ps 145:10 *All you have made will praise you, O LORD; your saints will extol you.*
NIV Ps 145:11 *They will tell of the glory of your kingdom and speak of your might,*
NIV Ps 145:12 *so that all men may know of your mighty acts and the glorious splendor of your kingdom.*
NIV Ps 145:13 *Your kingdom is an everlasting kingdom, and your dominion endures through all generations.*
The LORD is faithful to all his promises and loving toward all he has made.
NIV Ps 145:14 *The LORD upholds all those who fall and lifts up all who are bowed down.*
NIV Ps 145:15 *The eyes of all look to you, and you give them their food at the proper time.*
NIV Ps 145:16 *You open your hand and satisfy the desires of every living thing.*
NIV Ps 145:17 *The LORD is righteous in all his ways and loving toward all he has made.*
NIV Ps 145:18 *The LORD is near to all who call on him, to all who call on him in truth.*
NIV Ps 145:19 *He fulfills the desires of those who fear him; he hears their cry and saves them.*
NIV Ps 145:20 *The LORD watches over all who love him, but all the wicked he will destroy.*

God knew that man had a hopeless inability to relate to Him in a manner in which He could fulfill His promises to bless them; nevertheless, He still promised. Then He made a blood oath, swearing to fulfill those promises.

Because of how the blood oath was structured, God makes Himself responsible when His promises go unfulfilled, even though it was a defect on man's part which disqualified him from receiving the promises God swore He would give. This happened because there were blessings and curses put on God's laws which disqualify man from receiving the blessings of His promises if they do not keep them. In essence man has rejected receiving the promises God swore to give, causing God to pay the consequences.

Therefore and because of how the blood oath was structured, when man inevitably failed at using the law to comply with the will of God and in doing so reconcile with Him, it does not bring any consequences upon man's head according to that blood oath God made. Man pays no price other than to go on being unreconciled with God and fit only for eventual destruction, making himself unworthy of the blessed promises. In other words, the children of the promise made themselves subject to the curses by virtue of making themselves unfit for the promises. However, according to the oath, the Lord must pay consequences because of how He swore that He would if He did not keep His promises.

The Lord was patient with the children of the promise from the beginning when they entered into the land of promise. After every chance was extended and rejected, God sent Babylon to destroy their cities and carry them out of the beautiful land pressing them back into forced servitude once again. He gave them over to Babylon for 70 years. The purpose was to be under forced servitude once again, giving them a refresher's course (if you will) in an effort to soften up their hearts so they might once again have the capacity to serve His will and not their own.

Note: The Lord often referred to Israel as a "stiff-necked people." This is because the neck, which can turn the head any direction, is a metaphor for the will of man. In addition to that, when a plowman would plow with a yoke of oxen, he would prod the lead oxen to go in the direction he wanted by poking him on the side of his neck with a sharp stick. It is the same when riding a horse. To cause the horse to go in the direction the rider wishes, he pulls on the reins which bends his neck and faces his head in the direction he desires. When an ox would not respond to this technique they were said to have had, "a hard neck." Worded in translation as "stiff-necked." By calling them "stiff-necked" the Lord is saying about them that they are stubborn and willful people, unwilling to serve the will of God by inferring that their callousness (hardness) makes it almost impossible to prod into the right direction the will of the Jews through forced servitude. Even so, these children of His friend Abraham were more willing to serve the will of God than the balance of mankind had been willing.

He turned His face away from their willful disobedience in doing so. At the end of those 70 years, the Lord turned towards them once again. He gave them an opportunity to return to the beautiful land and once again serve Him. However, from then until this day and beyond, the Lord has not released them to be entirely free from Babylon's rule and threats. It will be that way until Jesus returns.

What He did do along with letting them return was give them 70-7 year periods broken up into three different times. Those 70-7's were given with the purpose of giving them a time of grace in which they could get rid of sin, finally lining up with and serving the Lord's will. Or to mount sin up so high that reconciliation with the Lord becomes impossible. In which case would cause the Lord to take other actions, including having to pay the consequences of His oath reconciling the Old Covenant as completed and to then put into effect a New Covenant. In the other case, He would have begun His kingdom with the children of the promise as His subjects. That is why when He was here He preached, "The Kingdom of God is at hand." According to the 70-7's, His Kingdom was meant to have begun seven years after the time of His death (the 70th-7) had they embraced Him instead of killed Him.

In either case and because 70-7's was the time allotted, He personally came to them in the person of Jesus ready for either contingency, but working only towards the one, which was to bless them and fulfill His promises. He stated when He was here that He came only to the children of Israel—the children of the promise. He tried to bless them exclusively; He healed them, bound up their wounds, fed them, comforted them, and gave them deliverance from their torments. He ordered His Apostles to only go to the children of Israel. It was only after He was rejected by them and killed did He commission the Apostles to go out to the whole world.

However, the Jews, thinking they were pious and observant of the law, were found to not be reconciled with Him but in grave opposition towards the Lord. They were unspiritual, and defective in fulfilling the spiritual aspects of the law (the righteous requirements of the law Ro 8:4). They rejected Him, and killed Him.

Amp Da 9:24 *Seventy weeks [of years, or 490 years] are decreed upon your people and upon your holy city [Jerusalem], to finish and put an end to transgression, to seal up and make full the measure of sin, to purge away and make expiation and reconciliation for sin, to bring in everlasting righteousness (permanent moral and spiritual rectitude in every area and relation) to seal up vision and prophecy and prophet, and to anoint a Holy of Holies.* (The baptism of Jesus)

Note: When it says, "are decreed upon your people and upon your holy city [Jerusalem] . . ." the word "decree" is important. When it is used in relation to something the Lord is saying, it denotes a judgment and sentence, as if the gavel has gone down. These 70-7's, as wonderful and generous as they are, is a judgment against the Israelites and against the people of the world. It is generous in that there is a specific time period that the Israelites are given to reconcile themselves with God just as a criminal would receive a sentence to serve time in jail. Yet the purpose of this time served is to either be found rehabilitated or found beyond redemption. Within the sentence which has a designated time limit is every opportunity allotted for them to reconcile themselves to God before the end of that time period. There is a contingency for either circumstances. It is to either "finish and put an end to transgression," or "make full the measure of sin."

He, the Lord, gave them long enough. He held out forgiveness long enough to prove they would not reconcile with Him nor stop rejecting His promises through noncompliance with His will and law.

NIV Mt 18:21 *Then Peter came to Jesus and asked, "Lord, how many times shall I forgive my brother when he sins against me? Up to seven times?"*
NIV Mt 18:22 *Jesus answered, "I tell you, not seven times, but seventy-seven times.*

The Lord did not hesitate, but submitted to the consequences of His unkept blood oath. He allowed them to show their unwillingness to reconcile by killing Him, and He thereby took responsibility for their defect, which disallowed His promises to be kept. The innocent God took responsibility and paid the consequences, so that guilty man would not have to pay the consequences and be destroyed forever. God knew that the only way He could accomplish His promises was for Him to endure those consequences. That is to say, He knowingly and undeservedly took on the responsibility for the sinful defect in man simply by making such an unkeepable oath. He now became responsible for man's future.

Having made this oath, which put the responsibility on Himself, He was then able to keep His promise to Noah as well. That is by not destroying all of mankind, who was ripe only for destruction. The Lord indeed is honorable! He not only made a rock so large He could not pick it up, but having done so He then made a way to pick it up. Through His death, He brought completion to the Old Covenant ending it, and at the same time—with the same act—He fulfilled the New Covenant.

When He died, it released His Spirit for us to ingest into ours. He therefore kept His promise to Eve (Gen 3:15). It is so important to understand the dual accomplishments His death achieved. In paying the price of nullifying the Old Covenant, God died the death we were deserving of. It is in this way He died for our sins. However, that same death gave us what we needed to overcome our defect—His Spirit and wisdom to perceive through.

Understanding all this about the purpose of the 70-7's helps us relate to the turmoil and disturbedness which must have been in Jesus' heart. He came here with a heart to bless them and begin His Kingdom with them. However, they would not have it; they rejected His blessings. This causes His promises to go unfulfilled, and because they would not receive His blessings (a good thing), He had to pay the consequences of His oath (an underserved cruel death).

However, knowing this would be the case, He used their rejection as a way to save the very ones who hated Him and rejected His blessings. He had to subject Himself to their hatred in order to help them. If they could have only aligned with His will by mastering the sin within, as the Lord admonished them to do, His death would not have been necessary. When He is faced with the reality of the finality of their decision to despise His do-or-die determination to bless them, He resigns to the fact that He must pay for His failed attempt to bless them in order to keep His word and bless them.

What a moment this must have been for Him, the Creator of all things! He had only one way left to keep His promise, and that was to fail at keeping His promise . . . By failing to keep His promise, He kept His promise. How can a soul bear the burden He carried? Listen to His agony over this moment when fate was finally sealed over this dilemma and there was no turning back:

Amp Mt 23:37 *O Jerusalem, Jerusalem, murdering the prophets and stoning those who are sent to you! How often would I have gathered your children together as a mother fowl gathers her brood under her wings, and you refused!*

Amp Mt 23:38 Behold, your house is forsaken and desolate (abandoned and left destitute of God's help).

Amp Mt 23:39 For I declare to you, you will not see Me again until you say, Blessed (magnified in worship, adored, and exalted) is He Who comes in the name of the Lord!

Amp Jn 12:27 Now My soul is troubled and distressed, and what shall I say? Father, save Me from this hour [of trial and agony]? But it was for this very purpose that I have come to this hour [that I might undergo it].

Amp Jn 12:28 [Rather, I will say,] Father, glorify (honor and extol) Your [own] name! Then there came a voice out of heaven saying, I have already glorified it, and I will glorify it again.

Amp Jn 12:29 The crowd of bystanders heard the sound and said that it had thundered; others said, An angel has spoken to Him!

Amp Jn 12:30 Jesus answered, This voice has not come for My sake, but for your sake.

Amp Jn 12:31 Now the judgment (crisis) of this world is coming on [sentence is now being passed on this world]. Now the ruler (evil genius, prince) of this world shall be cast out (expelled).

Amp Jn 12:32 And I, if and when I am lifted up from the earth [on the cross], will draw and attract all men [Gentiles as well as Jews] to Myself.

NIV Mt 26:36 Then Jesus went with his disciples to a place called Gethsemane, and he said to them, "Sit here while I go over there and pray."

NIV Mt 26:37 He took Peter and the two sons of Zebedee along with him, and he began to be sorrowful and troubled.

NIV Mt 26:38 Then he said to them, "My soul is overwhelmed with sorrow to the point of death. Stay here and keep watch with me."

NIV Mt 26:39 Going a little farther, he fell with his face to the ground and prayed, "My Father, if it is possible, may this cup be taken from me. Yet not as I will, but as you will."

NIV Mt 26:40 Then he returned to his disciples and found them sleeping. "Could you men not keep watch with me for one hour?" he asked Peter.

NIV Mt 26:41 *"Watch and pray so that you will not fall into temptation. The spirit is willing, but the body is weak."*

NIV Mt 26:42 *He went away a second time and prayed, "My Father, if it is not possible for this cup to be taken away unless I drink it, may your will be done."*

NIV Mt 26:43 *When he came back, he again found them sleeping, because their eyes were heavy.*

NIV Mt 26:44 *So he left them and went away once more and prayed the third time, saying the same thing.*

NIV Mt 26:45 *Then he returned to the disciples and said to them, "Are you still sleeping and resting? Look, the hour is near, and the Son of Man is betrayed into the hands of sinners.*

NIV Mt 26:46 *Rise, let us go! Here comes my betrayer!"*

Luke's account of the same event:

NIV Lk 22:39 *Jesus went out as usual to the Mount of Olives, and his disciples followed him.*

NIV Lk 22:40 *On reaching the place, he said to them, "Pray that you will not fall into temptation."*

NIV Lk 22:41 *He withdrew about a stone's throw beyond them, knelt down and prayed,*

NIV Lk 22:42 *"Father, if you are willing, take this cup from me; yet not my will, but yours be done."*

NIV Lk 22:43 *An angel from heaven appeared to him and strengthened him.*

NIV Lk 22:44 *And being in anguish, he prayed more earnestly, and his sweat was like drops of blood falling to the ground.*

NIV Lk 22:45 *When he rose from prayer and went back to the disciples, he found them asleep, exhausted from sorrow.*

NIV Lk 22:46 *"Why are you sleeping?" he asked them. "Get up and pray so that you will not fall into temptation."*

It is a prophetic picture to take note that His disciples were sleeping at the most definitive moment in history. He not only has taken the responsibility for our defect, suffering the consequences for it, but paid the price for us to be delivered from it. All while He is doing this incredibly sacrificial thing for our benefit, we are asleep, in the fog, oblivious, and under the spell of our defect, causing Him to have to do it all.

. . . Truly He is a kind and generous God!

Pause

Epilogue

It must be asked, how can He defeat and expel the Devil, casting him out of the world, by letting the agents of the Devil kill Him? What kind of judgment and sentence is that on the world? And if He came here to provide a power to overcome the defect, why is He saying that it's about defeating the Devil and casting him out and bringing sentence on him?

Amp Jn 9:39 Then Jesus said, I came into this world for judgment [as a Separator, in order that there may be separation between those who believe on Me and those who reject Me], to make the sightless see and to make those who see become blind.

It is more simple than one can imagine! Here is a question many of us ask, "Why does God hold me responsible and condemn me for a choice Adam and Eve made?" Here is another verse Jesus was quoted as saying:

NIV Lk 12:49 "I have come to bring fire on the earth, and how I wish it were already kindled!
NIV Lk 12:50 But I have a baptism to undergo, and how distressed I am until it is completed!¹
NIV Lk 12:51 Do you think I came to bring peace on earth? No, I tell you, but division.
NIV Lk 12:52 From now on there will be five in one family divided against each other, three against two and two against three.

NIV Lk 12:53 *They will be divided, father against son and son against father, mother against daughter and daughter against mother, mother-in-law against daughter-in-law and daughter-in-law against mother-in-law."*

NIV Lk 12:54 *He said to the crowd: "When you see a cloud rising in the west, immediately you say, 'It's going to rain,' and it does.*

NIV Lk 12:55 *And when the south wind blows, you say, 'It's going to be hot,' and it is.*

NIV Lk 12:56 *Hypocrites! You know how to interpret the appearance of the earth and the sky. How is it that you don't know how to interpret this present time?*

NIV Lk 12:57 *"Why don't you judge for yourselves what is right?*

Adam and Eve chose to bind their human spirit to the spirit of the Devil over that of God's. That choice corrupted the human spirit and its wisdom, and through that choice, death entered into the world. To do what they did was their choice, not ours. One could say we are victims of their choice. However, by Jesus coming into the world as God incarnate, then dividing people who would follow Him from those who would remain as they are, is to give us the same choice Adam and Eve had. This is what He was referring to when He said they could not read the signs of the times. It's time to choose so we may be judged by our own choice, not Adam and Eve's. We need to judge for ourselves which choice is right.

NIV Jn 9:39 *Jesus said, "For judgment I have come into this world, so that the blind will see and those who see will become blind."*

NIV Jn 9:40 *Some Pharisees who were with him heard him say this and asked, "What? Are we blind too?"*

NIV Jn 9:41 *Jesus said, "If you were blind, you would not be guilty of sin; but now that you claim you can see, your guilt remains.*

NIV Jn 15:22 *If I had not come and spoken to them, they would not be guilty of sin. Now, however, they have no excuse for their sin.*

NIV Jn 15:23 *He who hates me hates my Father as well.*

NIV Jn 15:24 *If I had not done among them what no one else did, they would not be guilty of sin. But now they have seen these miracles, and yet they have hated both me and my Father.*

NIV Jn 15:25 *But this is to fulfill what is written in their Law: 'They hated me without reason.'*

Through no fault of our own, Adam and Eve chose to bind themselves to the spirit of the Devil in rebellion to God. The One God has come, and He presents to us a choice. To follow Him, showing ourselves not in agreement with the decision of Adam and Eve, or to remain the same as them in defiance and rebellion to God, thereby endorsing their decision.

Jesus says, we are children of wrath because of what Adam and Eve chose and are perceiving life according to their choice, but since it was not us who made that choice, He considers us innocent. However, because of the judgment of fire which is already in progress, it is time to make a choice because the earth is being condemned with fire. If we choose to follow Him, we will remain innocent as one who is in disagreement with that awful decision in the garden—we will save our lives. However, if we choose to reject Jesus, being that we are already children of wrath, the guilt of Adam and Eve for rebelling and defying God remains on us and we "remain guilty." We remain just as guilty as them, and therefore remain the subjects of His judgment of fire. All things considered, it becomes our decision (not Adam and Eve's) to eat the fruit of the knowledge of good and evil as opposed to the bread of life. We then are found deserving to perish in the lake of fire based on our own merit.

The spirit and wisdom of the Devil ingested and simulated into the human spirit in the garden has ruled and held in bondage the perception of the human spirit ever since. It created a defect which does not allow man to reconcile with God even if he desires. For Jesus, being God, to come and, through His death, release His disembodied Spirit with His wisdom values for the human heart to ingest, is to expel and cast out the spirit and wisdom of the Devil one person at a time. In this way, the Devil—his spirit and wisdom infested in the human spirit—is cast out, losing His power over us. It is the Devil's rule over our perception of life which Jesus came to pass sentence on.

Therefore, it is a new perception and power He came to give us so we might overcome our defect and be set free of our old one. And in giving us this power, we may cast out the power the Devil has over us. As such, it is indeed to cast out and defeat the Devil. The spirit of the Devil is the fruit of the knowledge of good and evil. The Spirit of Christ is the bread of life. We must eat His flesh and drink His blood to have eternal life. This is why Jesus is the only way! He was the tree of life in the garden and He was what Adam and Eve rejected. We can no longer say we are being condemned because of the choice of Adam and Eve. He has come to face everyone with that same choice!

Amp Eph 1:17 *[For I always pray to] the God of our Lord Jesus Christ, the Father of glory, that He may grant you a spirit of wisdom and revelation [of insight into mysteries and secrets] in the [deep and intimate] knowledge of Him,*

Eph 1:18 *By having the eyes of your heart flooded with light, so that you can know and understand the hope to which He has called you, and how rich is His glorious inheritance in the saints (His set-apart ones),*

Amp Eph 1:19 *And [so that you can know and understand] what is the immeasurable and unlimited and surpassing greatness of His power in and for us who believe, as demonstrated in the working of His mighty strength,*

Amp Eph 1:20 *Which He exerted in Christ when He raised Him from the dead and seated Him at His [own] right hand in the heavenly [places],*

Amp Eph 1:21 *Far above all rule and authority and power and dominion and every name that is named [above every title that can be conferred], not only in this age and in this world, but also in the age and the world which are to come.*

Amp Eph 1:22 *And He has put all things under His feet and has appointed Him the universal and supreme Head of the church [a headship exercised throughout the church],*

Amp Eph 1:23 Which is His body, the fullness of Him Who fills all in all [for in that body lives the full measure of Him Who makes everything complete, and Who fills everything everywhere with Himself]. (Fills everything with His disembodied Spirit)

Amp Eph 2:1 AND YOU [He made alive], when you were dead (slain) by [your] trespasses and sins

Amp Eph 2:2 In which at one time you walked [habitually]. You were following the course and fashion of this world [were under the sway of the tendency of this present age], following the prince of the power of the air. [You were obedient to and under the control of] the [demon] spirit that still constantly works in the sons of disobedience [the careless, the rebellious, and the unbelieving, who go against the purposes of God].

Amp Eph 2:3 Among these we as well as you once lived and conducted ourselves in the passions of our flesh [our behavior governed by our corrupt and sensual nature], obeying the impulses of the flesh and the thoughts of the mind [our cravings dictated by our senses and our dark imaginings]. We were then by nature children of [God's] wrath and heirs of [His] indignation, like the rest of mankind.

Amp Eph 2:4 But God—so rich is He in His mercy! Because of and in order to satisfy the great and wonderful and intense love with which He loved us,

Amp Eph 2:5 Even when we were dead (slain) by [our own] shortcomings and trespasses, He made us alive together in fellowship and in union with Christ; [He gave us the very life of Christ Himself (His Spirit), the same new life with which He quickened Him, for] it is by grace (His favor and mercy which you did not deserve) that you are saved (delivered from judgment and made partakers of Christ's salvation).

Amp Eph 2:6 And He raised us up together with Him and made us sit down together [giving us joint seating with Him] in the heavenly sphere [by virtue of our being] in Christ Jesus (the Messiah, the Anointed One).

Amp Eph 2:7 He did this that He might clearly demonstrate through the ages to come the immeasurable (limitless, surpassing) riches of His free grace (His unmerited favor) in [His] kindness and goodness of heart toward us in Christ Jesus.

Amp Eph 2:8 *For it is by free grace (God's unmerited favor) that you are saved (delivered from judgment and made partakers of Christ's salvation) through [your] faith. And this [salvation] is not of yourselves [of your own doing, it came not through your own striving], but it is the gift of God;*

Amp Eph 2:9 *Not because of works [not the fulfillment of the Law's demands], lest any man should boast. [It is not the result of what anyone can possibly do, so no one can pride himself in it or take glory to himself.]*

This defect is so profound that it makes it impossible to conform to God, then be reconciled.

If God would subject Himself to the unthinkable in order to empower us to overcome that defect instead of giving up on us and destroying us all, then it would be reasonable to believe our religion should be centered around efforts to use that overcoming power to rise above that defect. Then finally we can correct the problem the defect would not allow us to correct. Otherwise, as the Bible states:

Amp 2Ti 3:5 *For [although] they hold a form of piety (true religion), they deny and reject and are strangers to the power of it [their conduct belies the genuineness of their profession].*

CHAPTER 4

Overcoming the Defect

Now knowing that to overcome the defect allows us to correct the problem, the question remains, "What is the problem?" Man cannot reconcile with God until he spiritually conforms to the will of God (which means in his perception, intents, and motives [his spirit nature]). To be reconciled, man needs to become a lover of God serving Him above loving and serving himself and his own desires. There is so much more to being reconciled to God than to become a more generous and better person.

Again, what is the defect which prevents us from correcting the problem?

The defect is simple; it is the values by which we perceive through, our world view, known in the Bible as our "wisdom." Because of our sin nature, man, in his essence, does not have the power within himself to love and obey God in a way that his love and obedience actually serves something other than his own personal purposes, will, and desires. At best, we can at times behaviorally conform to God's laws, but only in a way which serves self and not God. This makes it impossible to truly conform to God and then be reconciled. Simply because at the end, we are not serving God but instead serving ourselves even by our obedience to the behavioral aspect of the law. Paul summed up that defect by calling the man afflicted with it as being, "unspiritual." Again, as possessing the "spirit of this world," or the "wisdom of this world."

Given its importance towards our eternal life, let us start by looking deeper at this defect. Paul expounds upon the defect of man's human spirit being reconciled with God through the commandments. He shows the impossibility of man to conform to the spiritual aspect and demands of the law which he calls, the "righteous requirements of the law." This inability is what makes him unspiritual. Paul realizes, as with all men, he can only conform to the law in an outward behavioral sense, but falls miserably short of conforming to the spiritual demands of the same law. Furthermore, because of his spiritual defect he fails at the behavioral codes too, when all is said and done. This is because in the center of who we are we are bent on serving our own will—we are lovers of ourselves. These two factors add up to our sin nature; it is the spirit fused with ours which has corrupted the human spirit.

Struggling With Sin

NIV Ro 7:7 *What shall we say, then? Is the law sin? Certainly not! Indeed I would not have known what sin was except through the law. For I would not have known what coveting really was if the law had not said, "Do not covet."*

NIV Ro 7:8 *But sin, seizing the opportunity afforded by the commandment, produced in me every kind of covetous desire. For apart from law, sin is dead.*

NIV Ro 7:9 *Once I was alive apart from law; but when the commandment came, sin sprang to life and I died.*

NIV Ro 7:10 *I found that the very commandment that was intended to bring life actually brought death.*

NIV Ro 7:11 *For sin, seizing the opportunity afforded by the commandment, deceived me, and through the commandment put me to death.*

Note: This is an important revelation of Paul's in verses 8 through 11. He is helping us see that to conform to the law doesn't just mean to behave outwardly within its boundaries. When he wants to serve God by keeping the law (which was meant to cause him to serve the Lord's will), the leeway the law gives him to do an act, he takes advantage of, and does so in order to serve himself and carry out his own self-serving will, purposes, and desires.

In his heart, he does not act on what the law allows with the intent and motive to serve the Lord's purposes, will and desires, but his own. As such, his sinful nature takes advantage of the law as permission to act with a sinful intent (which is to serve self not God). He has broken the first and last commandments using the behavioral codes as a rationale to do so. He goes on in the verses to come showing how futile it is, because he is unspiritual and has an inability to conform to the law in a spiritual way. Which, if were possible, would result in true conformity to God leading to true reconciliation with Him.

NIV Ro 7:12 *So then, the law is holy, and the commandment is holy, righteous and good.*

NIV Ro 7:13 *Did that which is good, then, become death to me? By no means! But in order that sin might be recognized as sin, it produced death in me through what was good, so that through the commandment sin might become utterly sinful.*

NIV Ro 7:14 *We know that the law is spiritual; but I am unspiritual, sold as a slave to sin.*

Ro 7:15 *I do not understand what I do. For what I want to do I do not do, but what I hate I do.*

NIV Ro 7:16 *And if I do what I do not want to do, I agree that the law is good.*

NIV Ro 7:17 *As it is, it is no longer I myself who do it, but it is sin living in me.*

NIV Ro 7:18 *I know that nothing good lives in me, that is, in my sinful nature. For I have the desire to do what is good, but I cannot carry it out.*

NIV Ro 7:19 *For what I do is not the good I want to do; no, the evil I do not want to do—this I keep on doing.*

NIV Ro 7:20 *Now if I do what I do not want to do, it is no longer I who do it, but it is sin living in me that does it.*

NIV Ro 7:21 *So I find this law at work: When I want to do good, evil is right there with me.*

NIV Ro 7:22 *For in my inner being I delight in God's law;*

NIV Ro 7:23 *but I see another law at work in the members of my body, waging war against the law of my mind and making me a prisoner of the law of sin at work within my members.*

NIV Ro 7:24 *What a wretched man I am! Who will rescue me from this body of death?*

NIV Ro 7:25 *Thanks be to God—through Jesus Christ our Lord! So then, I myself in my mind am a slave to God's law, but in the sinful nature a slave to the law of sin.*

Paul hits the problem right on the head! He recognizes the defect that God found with us which made the first Covenant (the commandments) ineffective in saving and reconciling us to Him. However, God did find a way, through the law, to help us see about ourselves the sinful spirit within. That spirit is right there present within us ready to use all things, good and bad/right and wrong, taking advantage of all things in order to have expression to serve ourselves. For Paul realized that even though he loved God and His law, he would not serve the purpose he wanted in obeying the law. Something within, something foreign, the sinful nature of his corrupt human spirit would do the right thing for the wrong reason and thereby serve the sin within him and not God, who he desired to serve (That is, who following the law was meant to serve).

He calls himself a slave because, by nature, what a slave does is serve his master. If he is in bondage to sin, everything he does, even his attempts to obey the law, serves the Devil, and therefore he is a slave to the Devil, his master. However, if what he does with his life serves righteousness, that, in turn, makes him a slave to righteousness. For again, whatever master you serve makes you a slave to that master.

Again, instead of serving God's purposes and will, making Him the true center of all things, we use the commands in a way to have an outward appearance of conformity while at the same time a justification to serve our own will and desires. As it turns out, we cannot do the right things for the right reasons. Almost without exception, the things we do, we do because in the end they somehow serve our own interest.

We would like to believe that we are killing two birds with one stone by doing things that serve both God and self or serve others and self. However, in the spiritual or heavenly dichotomy this is not pure and falls short of honoring the Lord's will in a truly holistic way. In reality, when it comes down to it, this heart posture will forever have to choose giving preference to one above the other. The reality is that to serve one means to dishonor the other. This is why Jesus tells all of Christianity:

Amp Rev 2:4 *But I have this [one charge to make] against you: that you have left (abandoned) the love that you had at first [you have deserted Me, your first love].*

And again Jesus said:

NIV Lk 16:13 *"No servant can serve two masters. Either he will hate the one and love the other, or he will be devoted to the one and despise the other. . . . .*

"Sin, seizing the opportunity afforded by the commandments, produced in me every kind of covetous desire." We break the first and last commandments when we use the laws of God to fulfill our own purposes and desires. We mock and betray the Spirit of the law when we do this, as if the Lord is a fool and doesn't know we are using His laws meant to serve Him as a way to serve ourselves.

Amp Gal 6:7 *Do not be deceived and deluded and misled; God will not allow Himself to be sneered at (scorned, disdained, or mocked by mere pretensions or professions, or by His precepts being set aside.) [He inevitably deludes himself who attempts to delude God.] For whatever a man sows, that and that only is what he will reap.*

Amp Gal 6:8 *For he who sows to his own flesh (lower nature, sensuality) will from the flesh reap decay and ruin and destruction, but he who sows to the Spirit will from the Spirit reap eternal life.*

When it says, "he who sows to his own flesh," he is talking about the purposes one has in his heart for doing a thing—what his efforts are directed towards accomplishing. It is for that thing one's efforts will benefit or nurture. Every decision and act one commits to, can serve God or self. Serve your standing in the spirit, or your standing in the world. The determining factor is whether you have in mind to benefit and nurture your life in this world (being a lover of self), or to benefit and nurture your relationship with God—honoring Him (God being your first love). Paul categorizes the two as either sowing into the flesh (unspiritual) or sowing into the Spirit (spiritual or to be "a spiritual man"). This is exactly the point Jesus is trying to make when He spoke the following words:

NIV Mt 6:16 *"When you fast, do not look somber as the hypocrites do, for they disfigure their faces to show men they are fasting. I tell you the truth, they have received their reward in full.* (to get praise and esteem from other men)
NIV Mt 6:17 *But when you fast, put oil on your head and wash your face,*
NIV Mt 6:18 *so that it will not be obvious to men that you are fasting, but only to your Father, who is unseen; and your Father, who sees what is done in secret, will reward you.*
NIV Mt 6:19 *"Do not store up for yourselves treasures on earth, where moth and rust destroy, and where thieves break in and steal.*
NIV Mt 6:20 *But store up for yourselves treasures in heaven, where moth and rust do not destroy, and where thieves do not break in and steal.*
NIV Mt 6:21 *For where your treasure is, there your heart will be also.*

In Gal 6:8 Paul says this: "For he who sows to his own flesh (lower nature, sensuality) will from the flesh reap decay and ruin and destruction, but he who sows to the Spirit will from the Spirit reap eternal life." One may ask that if you sow or invest into your flesh, your lower nature, why is it automatic that you will reap or get a return on your investment of decay, ruin, and destruction? It's really very simple. For example, say you live in these modern times when computers first hit the market. You saw it as a good thing and you invested all you had in computer products and software. You would have had a huge return on your investment. You have invested in something that will pay off in the future, simply because computers are the future, and you will have an ongoing benefit as a result.

However, let's say you lived in past times and were on a luxury passenger liner called, the Titanic, traveling on its maiden voyage on the ocean between England and the United States. You invested all you had in purchasing stock in the future of this brand new ocean liner. In doing so, you would come to find out your return would be nothing and bear no fruit for you. It would only bring ruin and death to you. Why? Because the ship sunk in the ocean and was destroyed and almost everyone aboard died.

Knowing in advance that computers would be the future, likewise, knowing in advance that this brand new luxury liner would sink to the ocean floor would be really great information before deciding to invest all that you have. It is like this when we make a decision to sow and invest into our flesh in this present world. All of the Apostles knew because of the teachings of Jesus that this world has an irrevocable death sentence on it and will be destroyed. In addition, this physical body will die as well. They understand there is no future in this present world. Your investment in it will yield or reap only ruin, death, and destruction. This is a fact and the judgment of God.

At the same time, they know the world to come will bring life eternal and relief from the decay of this world. This is a huge return for your investment if you should give all that you have towards living for the world to come. However, those who invest all that they are into getting a return in this present world, in their current body, are going to receive for their investment the same as the man on the Titanic. As said above, knowing in advance the return on what you spend your life on gives the smart investor all he needs to know before he invests.

Paul is simply giving us the facts. Here is your inside trading information: Spend your life on seeking comfort and happiness in this present world and, as sure as what happened to the Titanic, your return will be decay, ruin, and destruction. Spend your life on living for the world to come, and your reward will be life eternal. The latter simply is a better investment. Paul constantly put things in these terms, and the truth is, nothing could be more accurate.

This single defect of being unspiritual so that we can serve self and not God is by far the most common sin we commit in almost every decision and deed. However, it is the one sin we do not repent of, or do so the least. Paul said, "We know that the law is spiritual; but I am unspiritual, sold as a slave to sin." The wisdom values and perception of our corrupt spirit is unspiritual and of the Devil and serves self. We judge, understand, and perceive everything as if we are god—how all things effect and serve us as if we are the center of all things. It falsifies the truth and is blind to the spiritual, which is that God is the center of all things, and it is His will and purposes which prevail and we ultimately serve.

As a result of our defect of being unspiritual in our wisdom, it makes what Paul says true: there is something inside us which rises up and uses what is good for the evil we don't really want to serve—self. We are slaves to that thing within. That thing is our master, and we are hopelessly under its power. Whatever we try to do (good or bad), in the end what we do ends up always serving our master, sin.

To bring this point home, you could say in another way that when self is our first love, then our master is self, which is sin. With self/sin being our master, then no matter what we do (good or bad) we do it to serve self (our master). So Paul cries out, "What a wretched man I am! Who will rescue me from this body of death? Thanks be to God—through Jesus Christ our Lord!"

Without a new spirit which delights in obedience towards God, and has spiritual wisdom values, we are inapt in trying to conform to the law both in its purpose and its practices. This being the case, as Hebrews points out, God made a New Covenant which, in effect, annulled the first.

Therefore, the next questions that must be asked are: What is the New Covenant? What is this power? What are its promises? How does it solve the problem by first overcoming the defect that the Old Covenant showed us about ourselves? Most importantly, how does it cause us to have a new master so that when we try to do good it actually serves good and not the evil within us, which before was our master? Finally, how can it make us spiritual men and women?

Having entered into a New Covenant relationship with Christ, we must focus on the advantage and overcoming power it has over the defect in us outwardly following the law that Moses gave. Otherwise, we are not addressing the real issues or doing anything more about what rules our souls than those who struggled with sin before the New Covenant power to overcome was released.

Note: Ask about the promises, blessings, and curses of the law in the Old Covenant and there is a significant percentage of Christians who can give a reasonable understanding of it. However, it is rare, even nonexistent, that Christians are taught what the promises of the New Covenant are, shockingly, even among pastors, scholars, and at seminary schools. It has been our experience that no answers are given when asked what the promises of the New Covenant are no matter who we approach. All people seem to understand is: Jesus died for our sins, and we live by faith and not by works, while not having a clarity of how that works or what that looks like. How can we live in a New Covenant relationship with Christ if we don't know what its promises are and what it is meant to help us accomplish?

Below are the verses in the Bible which tell us the promises of the New Covenant. These promises are the purpose Jesus' death served and accomplished.

The Statutes of the New Covenant

A covenant of the heart/conscience and no longer of the written word.

NIV Jer 31:33-34 *This is the covenant which I will make with the house of Israel after that time," declares the LORD. "I will put my law in their minds and write it on their hearts. I will be their God, and they will be my people ...*

NLT Eze 36:26a *I will give you a new heart with new and right desires*

NLT Eze 36:26b *I will take out your stony heart of sin and give you a new, obedient heart*

Amp Eze 11:19 *I will take the stony [unnaturally hardened] heart out of your flesh, and will give you a heart of flesh [sensitive and responsive to the touch of your God]*

Amp Isa 54:13 *And all your [spiritual] children shall be disciples [taught by the Lord and obedient to His will], and great shall be the peace and undisturbed composure of your children.*

Amp Jer 31:33-34 *I will put My law within you, and on your heart will I write it. They will no more teach each man his neighbor and each man his brother, saying, Know the Lord, for you will all know Me [recognize, understand, and be acquainted with Me], from the least of you to the greatest*

NLT Eze 36:25 *I will sprinkle clean water on you, and you will be clean. Your filth will be washed away . . .*

NLT Eze 36:29 *I will cleanse you of your filthy behavior.*

Amp Jer 31:34 *I will forgive your iniquity, and I will [seriously] remember your sin no more*

Amp Eze 36:26-27 *I will put a new spirit in you. I will put My Spirit within you and cause you to walk in My statutes, and you shall heed My ordinances and do them.*

If one is wondering how important these statutes of the New Covenant are to salvation as well as to the Christian experience, one only has to look as far as the concluding statement God Himself made concerning these statutes outlined above,

THUS SAITH THE LORD:

WEB Jer 31:35 *Yahweh, who gives the sun for a light by day,*
and the ordinances of the moon and of the stars for a light by night,
who stirs up the sea, so that its waves roar;
Yahweh of Armies is his name, says:
WEB Jer 31:36 *"If these ordinances depart from before me," says Yahweh,*
"then the offspring of Israel also will cease from being a nation before me forever."
WEB Jer 31:37 *Yahweh says: "If heaven above can be measured,*
and the foundations of the earth searched out beneath,

then I will also cast off all the offspring of Israel for all that they have done," says Yahweh.

What He is saying by these words is that without these New Covenant ordinances, which He is decreeing, Israel will not be able to be a nation, nor His people for eternity—they will perish with Babylon. In other words, because of their constant sinning and unspiritual hearts this is what it is going to take: Him teaching everyone personally and Him giving everyone His own Spirit that will cause them to finally obey Him both spiritually and behaviorally. Thus, with His Spirit, we will have a new master, and what we do will finally serve the good we want to serve and not the evil we do not want to serve. This is the only way for Him to be able to keep His promise that Israel will be His people forever.

Furthermore, He concludes by saying that in spite of their failure to keep the Old Covenant and their constant sinning against Him, there is a snowball's chance in the lake of fire that He will rescind the ordinances of the New Covenant. Nothing will prevent Him from personally teaching everyone and from giving His Spirit, even if it means He has to come in human form and die. This is how important it is for God to keep His word—this is how much He loves His people!

Who knew that for God to keep this promise of the New Covenant He would do so by paying the consequences of the Old going unfulfilled? Who, at the time these promises were made, would dream that in order to give us a new Spirit (a new master to serve) He would be required to personally come, be born, and die to release in the earth for all who desire His disembodied Spirit (the promised Spirit that would cause us to obey God)?

CHAPTER 5

A Closer Look at the New Covenant Promises

1) Cleansed of our filth and forgiven:

NLT Eze 36:25 *I will sprinkle clean water on you, and you will be clean. Your filth will be washed away . . .*

NLT Eze 36:29 *I will cleanse you of your filthy behavior.*

Amp Jer 31:34 *I will forgive your iniquity, and I will [seriously] remember your sin no more*

A saying we would remind ourselves of when laying hands on people is: "When Jesus touches dirt, His hands don't become dirty, the dirt becomes clean." When we take into our hearts His disembodied Spirit and His Spirit encounters our filthy heart (the Lord's word), He doesn't become infected, but our unclean spirit becomes clean. To become forgiven and cleansed is the first step in being convicted, in a spiritual sense, leading to reconciliation with the Lord.

2) Taught by God:

Amp Isa 54:13 *And all your [spiritual] children shall be disciples [taught by the Lord and obedient to His will], and great shall be the peace and undisturbed composure of your children.*

Amp Jer 31:33-34 *I will put My law within you, and on your heart will I write it. They will no more teach each man his neighbor and each man his brother, saying, Know the Lord, for you will all know Me [recognize, understand, and be acquainted with Me], from the least of you to the greatest*

NAS JN 1:18 *No one has seen God at any time; the only begotten God who is in the bosom of the Father, He has explained Him.*

The way that God Himself teaches us is twofold.

1) By His Spirit in us, He makes His will known to us, through our conscience, and helps us interpret His words.

Amp Jn 7:16 *Jesus answered them by saying, My teaching is not My own, but His Who sent Me.*
Amp Jn 7:17 *If any man desires to do His will (God's pleasure), he will know (have the needed illumination to recognize, and can tell for himself) whether the teaching is from God . . .*

This is an amazing answer when they questioned if Jesus was from God! Jesus turned it around on them, showing them that not knowing was actually an indictment against them. Jesus makes discerning God not a matter of intelligence or learning, but a matter of whom the heart desires to serve. John verifies this in his letters:

Amp 1Jn 4:6 *We are from God, and whoever knows God listens to us; but whoever is not from God does not listen to us. This is how we recognize the Spirit of truth and the spirit of falsehood.*

If they listen to us, we then know they are from God and they have the Spirit of truth. If they dismiss us, we know they don't have the Spirit of truth—the wisdom from heaven. Rather, they have the wisdom of this world, which is the spirit of falsehood. So they can build churches and talk as if they have every verse of the Bible memorized, but they give themselves away as ones who do not desire to serve God, but self.

If one fully desires to serve God and do His will (not his own), it will seem right in his heart when he hears something that comes from God. However, if one loves himself and desires to do his own will, carrying out his own agendas, what will seem right in his heart will be things which are in line with his own agendas and will. God's real words will, in fact, offend them, and because of their heart posture to serve self, they will react in a hostile or threatening way to God's words.

The learned men, the religious leaders of the Jews who questioned Jesus about His qualifications, and questioned if He spoke the words of God were indicting themselves as ones who serve themselves and not God. They may have thought they were showing their superior minds and great learning; however, by his response to them, Jesus was exposing them as not knowing God, not serving God. In fact, Jesus went on to say of them, "I know you, and there is no love of God in your hearts." He knew this simply by how they received Him and His words.

The point is that God's own Spirit does witness and confirm His true teachings in the hearts of those who desire to serve Him first before self. This is true also because the ones who want to serve Him before self have a different master than those of the religious leaders of the Jews. They wanted to serve self and use their position as religious leaders to do so.

2) The second is that He personally came here and taught us, giving us His Father's words and instructions. He taught us personally by coming among us. His teachings passed down to us are not teachings or theories of a mere man, a sage, scholar, philosopher, or saint. They are from God. God came to us and taught us Himself.

Amp Jn 14:9 *Jesus replied, Have I been with all of you for so long a time, and do you not recognize and know Me yet, Philip? Anyone who has seen Me has seen the Father. How can you say then, Show us the Father?*

Amp Jn 14:10 *Do you not believe that I am in the Father, and that the Father is in Me? What I am telling you I do not say on My own authority and of My own accord; but the Father Who lives continually in Me does the (His) works (His own miracles, deeds of power).*

Amp Jn 14:11 *Believe Me that I am in the Father and the Father in Me*

NIV Jn 17:20 *"My prayer is not for them alone. I pray also for those who will believe in me through their message,*

NIV Jn 17:21 *that all of them may be one, Father, just as you are in me and I am in you. May they also be in us so that the world may believe that you have sent me.*

John verifies (below) that the Christian teachings are not from men and their lofty ideas or theories, but from God personally who came down from heaven and taught us Himself through Jesus, and whose teachings were passed down to us by the Apostles.

Amp 1Jn 1:1 *[WE ARE writing] about the Word of Life [in] Him Who existed from the beginning, Whom we have heard, Whom we have seen with our [own] eyes, Whom we have gazed upon [for ourselves] and have touched with our [own] hands.*

Amp 1Jn 1:2 *And the Life [an aspect of His being] was revealed (made manifest, demonstrated), and we saw [as eyewitnesses] and are testifying to and declare to you the Life, the eternal Life [in Him] Who already existed with the Father and Who [actually] was made visible (was revealed) to us [His followers].*

Amp 1Jn 4:6 *We are from God, and whoever knows God listens to us; but whoever is not from God does not listen to us. This is how we recognize the Spirit of truth and the spirit of falsehood.*

Amp 1Jn 1:3 *What we have seen and [ourselves] heard, we are also telling you, so that you too may realize and enjoy fellowship as partners and partakers with us. And [this] fellowship that we have [which is a distinguishing mark of Christians] is with the Father and with His Son Jesus Christ (the Messiah).*

Amp 1Jn 1:4 *And we are now writing these things to you so that our joy [in seeing you included] may be full [and your joy may be complete].*

Amp 1Jn 1:5 *And this is the message [the message of promise] which we have heard from Him and now are reporting to you:*

Amp Jn 3:10 *Jesus replied, Are you the teacher of Israel, and yet do not know nor understand these things? [Are they strange to you?]*

Amp Jn 3:11 *I assure you, most solemnly I tell you, We speak only of what we know [we know absolutely what we are talking about]; we have actually seen what we are testifying to [we were eyewitnesses of it]. And still you do not receive our testimony [you reject and refuse our evidence—that of Myself and of all those who are born of the Spirit].*

Amp Jn 3:12 *If I have told you of things that happen right here on the earth and yet none of you believes Me, how can you believe (trust Me, adhere to Me, rely on Me) if I tell you of heavenly things?*

Amp Jn 3:13 *And yet no one has ever gone up to heaven, but there is One Who has come down from heaven—the Son of Man [Himself], Who is (dwells, has His home) in heaven.*

Note: It is interesting to take note that the four Gospels only speak what Jesus said and did along with some background to give context. In all four Gospels there is no attempt to interpret or explain what Jesus taught, said, or did. There is no commentary by the writers. They are simply four different accounts of what He spoke and taught in His own words. However, after the four Gospels, these same writers teach, interpret, and divide for us the teachings of Jesus. However, they do no such thing in presenting to us the Gospels.

It is obvious that they wanted us to hear the words of the Master Himself so that it is true that by reading them we too will have been personally taught by God just as the New Covenant promises. It is His teachings, unfiltered, that are shared with us through the four Gospels. God came here in the guise of human nature and taught us Himself. His eyewitness words are told to us by the writers of the Gospels.

3) A new Spirit:

Amp Eze 36:26-27 I will put a new spirit in you. I will put My Spirit within you and cause you to walk in My statutes, and you shall heed My ordinances and do them.

NIV Mk 1:8 I baptize you with water, but he will baptize you with the Holy Spirit."

NIV Jn 1:33 . . . the one who sent me to baptize with water told me, 'The man on whom you see the Spirit come down and remain is he who will baptize with the Holy Spirit.'
NIV Jn 1:34 I have seen and I testify that this is the Son of God."

In order for Jesus to give us a new Spirit, He has to be different than all who have been born of Adam.

What makes us an individual is our soul (or mind). Man, like God, is a triune being. All other created creatures are biune creatures. This means that both God and man have three natures: the spirit, soul, and body. The Holy Spirit is the Spirit of God, God or the Father is the soul or mind and will of God, and the Word of God (Jesus) is the embodiment of God.

NIV Jn 14:9 Jesus answered: "Don't you know me, Philip, even after I have been among you such a long time? Anyone who has seen me has seen the Father. How can you say, 'Show us the Father'?

NIV Jn 14:10 *Don't you believe that I am in the Father, and that the Father is in me? The words I say to you are not just my own. Rather, it is the Father, living in me, who is doing his work.*

NIV Jn 14:11 *Believe me when I say that I am in the Father and the Father is in me;*

Both angels and animals have only two natures: spirit and body. In addition, there are two different kinds of bodies: natural (or physical), and celestial. God, the angels, and other created celestial beings whose domain is in the spirit realm have celestial bodies made up of celestial matter. Human beings and animals whose domain is in the natural/physical realm have a natural body composed of physical matter.

Except God, no creature has an embodiment in each realm. That is notwithstanding the fact that some celestial creatures can manifest within the physical realm. However, it is still their celestial body we can view. All living creatures are either clothed with a celestial body, a physical body, or are naked. A deceased human is naked, a disembodied soul. A soul unclothed, unable to have an embodiment to give expression to its mind and to function within the realm he lives in.

We learn in the first chapter of John that the visible celestial embodiment of God is the Word (of God). We know from the Bible that the words God speaks come into being. Just as He created the universe by speaking it into existence, His words become manifest. As such, the Word of God is also the embodiment of God and clothes His invisible natures. His words give shape and form to everything, and His Spirit (the breath His words are carried on) give the power for His words to come into being/reality. In His celestial place, Jesus, the Word of God, is the embodiment of God. If you are in the spirit realm and you are gazing upon the image of God—His body—you are looking at the Word, who John identifies as one in the same as Jesus.

The Word of God came to us and manifested in a physical body in the person of Jesus. In essence, the outward manifestation of God has two bodies: one celestial and one physical. He also has two souls: one the Father and one the Son. However, they share the same Spirit, and that is what makes them One.

NIV Col 2:9 For in Christ all the fullness of the Deity lives in bodily form . . .

However, once Jesus departed from the natural world, He remained in the world as a disembodied Spirit—the Holy Spirit. Currently, His physical body in the natural world are all His followers who embody His Spirit (the Holy Spirit) and give expression to it through their life in the body. They collectively are the body of Christ—that is, if and when they obey His Spirit promptings. How we relate to Jesus in this way, making us one with Him, is in keeping with how Jesus relates to His Father making Him one with Him. He chooses to live for His Father's will and not His own.

NIV Jn 17:11 . . . so that they may be one as we are one.

NIV Jn 17:16 They are not of the world, even as I am not of it.

NIV Jn 17:21 that all of them may be one, Father, just as you are in me and I am in you. May they also be in us so that the world may believe that you have sent me.
NIV Jn 17:22 I have given them the glory that you gave me, that they may be one as we are one:
NIV Jn 17:23 I in them and you in me. May they be brought to complete unity to let the world know that you sent me and have loved them even as you have loved me.

NIV Jn 17:26 I have made you known to them, and will continue to make you known in order that the love you have for me may be in them and that I myself may be in them."

Paul tells us that the fullness of His Spirit is given expression to in the earth through the collective followers who embody Him by obeying His Spirit.

Amp Eph 1:22 *And He has put all things under His feet and has appointed Him the universal and supreme Head of the church [a headship exercised throughout the church],*
Amp Eph 1:23 *Which is His body, the fullness of Him Who fills all in all [for in that body lives the full measure of Him Who makes everything complete, and Who fills everything everywhere with Himself].*

Mathew and Luke give the human lineage of Jesus. It is only fitting that one Gospel, John, gives the spirit or celestial lineage of Jesus. It is fitting because Jesus was fully God and fully man, which means He actually has two different lineages (a celestial lineage, and a physical lineage). How do we know this? Jesus called Himself one of two things: (1) the Son of God (2) the Son of Man. It should be noted that when John gives the celestial lineage of Jesus, he calls Him the Word of God—the manifestation of God or the embodiment of God.

However, John refers to God in heaven as God, only until he gets to the part when he tells us that the Word of God became flesh and dwelt among us. After that event, John calls God in Heaven "the Father" and the Word of God, Jesus, "the Son of God." He does not call Him this before. Why? Because He became the Father of the only begotten Son, Jesus, at that time. Before, He was not a Father in that sense.

How can John and Jesus call God His Father? Because it is a fact that God is His Father! All humans born on earth have Adam as their father. The human spirit is the corrupt human spirit of Adam. All who are born of him possess not only his physical DNA, but his corrupted human spirit. It is the man's soul, his mind/personality, which makes him distinct from other humans.

The attributes of a soul are the will, the mind, the intellect, imagination, and emotions. The soul is the seat of decision, and of the man's reasoning. The soul is the real man.

God has promised us a new spirit and a new celestial body, replacing two of the three natures that comprise man. However, if God were to replace the soul, the man would not be the same man, he would cease to exist. For the soul is the real man.

NIV Jn 6:63 *The Spirit gives life, the flesh counts for nothing. The words I have spoken to you are spirit and they are life.*

That being the case, it says that God's Spirit doesn't replace the soul, but convicts and judges its thoughts and purposes in order to purify it and thus "salvage it." God's Spirit renews and cleanses, convicting our mind and reasoning in a way that causes us to think differently. This is because, by giving us His Spirit, He gives us new software—a new wisdom. However, it surgically cuts the soul free from the corrupt human spirit and flesh (the human body), giving the soul a new Spirit and eventually clothing it with a new and celestial body. We then become celestial humans. These are the three remedies of salvation for the three natures of a man. (1) We are born again with a new Spirit while forsaking the old, (2) we are given a resurrected celestial body dying to the old physical body, and (3) our soul/mind is salvaged by being renewed with a new spirit and wisdom. It is just as the verse (below) describes how salvation works for all three natures:

Heb 4:12 *For the Word that God speaks is alive and full of power [making it active, operative, energizing, and effective]; it is sharper than any two-edged sword, (1) penetrating to the dividing line of the breath of life (soul) and [the immortal] spirit, (2) and of joints and marrow (3) [of the deepest parts of our nature], exposing and sifting and analyzing and judging the very thoughts and purposes of the heart.*

Again, how can John and Jesus both call God, Jesus' Father?

To be a father, one has to impregnate a woman, creating a child. The one who provides the seed which fertilizes the egg, biologically speaking, is the father. Jesus' Father was God, because it was the Holy Spirit of God that impregnated Mary.

NIV Mt 1:20 *But after he had considered this, an angel of the Lord appeared to him in a dream and said, "Joseph son of David, do not be afraid to take Mary home as your wife, because what is conceived in her is from the Holy Spirit.*

In the truest definition of the word, God is the Father of Jesus. Jesus is the Son of God! Mary was a human born of the lineage of David. This makes Jesus also the Son of Man. Jesus is right to call Himself both. To do otherwise would be a lie.

Why point this out? To understand the New Covenant at all, it must be understood that Jesus was different than any other human being in the history of the world in that He was not born with, nor did He inherit, the corrupt human spirit of Adam. He was not born with the corrupt human spirit, but the Spirit of God—the Holy Spirit.

Amp Ro 8:3 *For God has done what the Law could not do, [its power] being weakened by the flesh [the entire nature of man without the Holy Spirit]. Sending His own Son in the guise of sinful flesh ...*

noun: guise; an external form, appearance, or manner of presentation, typically concealing the true nature of something.
Synonyms: likeness, outward appearance, appearance, semblance, form, shape, image, disguise; "he visited in the guise of an inspector"[1]

Jesus, in every way resembled a human. However, He is not a child of Adam. Yes, He is a triune being. He has a Spirit, soul, and body. Although the flesh He was clothed with was from Adam, His invisible natures were not. They were from God—they are God. If this were not true, spiritually He would have nothing to offer that was different than any other man was capable of offering.

Amp Jn 3:6 *What is born of [from] the flesh is flesh [of the physical is physical]; and what is born of the Spirit is spirit.*

It is because of this fact that Paul called Jesus the last Adam. Adam is the first source and father of the natural human race. Jesus, being the first and the (Spirit) source, making God the Father of a race of celestial humans. This is why Jesus admonished His followers to call no one on earth father, only God in heaven is their Father now. No more Adams are needed. The second Adam, Jesus, is the last Adam.

Amp 1Co 15:45 *Thus it is written, The first man Adam became a living being (an individual personality); the last Adam (Christ) became a life-giving Spirit [restoring the dead to life].*
Amp 1Co 15:46 *But it is not the spiritual life which came first, but the physical and then the spiritual.*
Amp 1Co 15:47 *The first man [was] from out of earth, made of dust (earthly-minded); the second Man [is] the Lord from out of heaven.*
Amp 1Co 15:48 *Now those who are made of the dust are like him who was first made of the dust (earthly-minded); and as is [the Man] from heaven, so also [are those] who are of heaven (heavenly-minded).*

Adam gave life to the human race of natural humans. Out of those humans and through a spiritual rebirth, Jesus gave the right to become celestial humans. Adam did so with his human spirit, and Jesus does so with His Heavenly Spirit.

It is wrong to think that Jesus received the Holy Spirit when He was baptized by John in the sense that He did not have the Holy Spirit before that, and was as all humans possessing the corrupt spirit of Adam. It makes Jesus God that His spirit is the Holy Spirit of God even if He is clothed in a human body. He did not become God after some test, but He was God. The word of God—the manifestation of God clothed in a human body!

NIV Da 9:24 "*Seventy 'sevens' are decreed for your people and your holy city to finish transgression, to put an end to sin, to atone for wickedness, to bring in everlasting righteousness, to seal up vision and prophecy and to anoint the most holy.*"

During the baptism by John, when the Spirit descended upon Him like a dove, it was the anointing of the most holy, spoken of in Daniel 9:24 (highlighted above). Like a ceremony or an inauguration (if you will) of Him becoming the high priest in the order of Melchizedek. It was then that He began His ministry and stepped into His destiny, fully approved and released by God (His Father) to carry out what He had come to earth to do. His destiny was to offer Himself as a sacrifice so that His disembodied Spirit (God's Spirit) would be spilled out upon the earth through His death, and man might ingest Him into their hearts, becoming one with Him.

NIV 2Co 4:7 But *we have this treasure* (the Holy Spirit) *in jars of clay* (in human bodies) *to show that this all-surpassing power is from God and not from us.*

Jesus was that earthen or clay vessel (natural body) broken open by His death, spilling out the contents of His now disembodied Spirit. That is the significance of the water and the blood which poured out of Him on the earth when He was pierced on the cross by the Roman soldier. Those who take His Spirit into their hearts, show their love for Him by obeying

His Spirit's every prompting. It is they who become the embodiment of Christ—His body—His bride.

Jesus was that clay pot of fire with a torch who swore a blood oath to His friend Abraham. The clay pot or earthen vessel represents the natural human body made from the earth. At the time the Word of God made the oath to His friend, He did not possess a human body made from the earth. That did not happen until He was born of Mary. The fire inside the pot was a representation of His Spirit—God's own Spirit within that earthen vessel (the human body of Jesus to come). The torch was, again, representative of something yet to come: humans who would embody His Spirit when He would make the sacrifice to come. The torch is the fire in the seven lampstands. And we who embody His Spirit carry that torch within us.

With the same act of paying the consequences for annulling the unkeepable Old Covenant and its promises, God also fulfilled the promise of the New Covenant. Both were accomplished by His death. He released His Spirit to man by becoming disembodied, and through death fulfilled the New Covenant promises of Him giving us His Spirit. At the same time and through His death, He paid the consequences of annulling the promises of His first covenant.

It was meant from the beginning, according to His long term plan, that the clay pot (Jesus) would be broken open as a sacrifice just like the animals sacrificed by being broken in two [and the blood spilled out in between].

NIV Ge 15:17 *When the sun had set and darkness had fallen, a smoking firepot with a blazing torch appeared and passed between the pieces.* (of animals)

In this way, the Lord kept His promise of the New Covenant when He said:

Amp Eze 36:26-27 *I will put a new spirit in you. I will put My Spirit within you and cause you to walk in My statutes, and you shall heed My ordinances and do them.*

NIV 1Co 1:30 *It is because of him that you are in Christ Jesus, who has become for us wisdom from God—that is, our righteousness, holiness and redemption.*

The Devil corrupted his wisdom; Adam and Eve envied his corrupted wisdom and ingested his spirit, infusing the God hating spirit of the Devil to their spirit in the process. Jesus, the bread of life, said, "You must eat my flesh (His words) and drink my blood (His Spirit) so you may have eternal life." Ingesting Jesus' Spirit gives a new and greater wisdom than what Adam started with in the first place. It is a wisdom from heaven that corrects our entire corrupted world view; a world view that is false to the true nature of life. It takes us from the lie of an "I, me, my" vision to the truth, which sets us free from that which makes us sin against God. It gives us a wisdom with values to perceive through which see God central to all things, and a heart to love Him in preference and through obedience. God becomes our first love, and no longer ourselves.

Notes

1 Guise. In *Oxford Dictionaries,* Retrieved May 2016, from
http://www.oxfordditionaries.com/us/definition/
american_english/guise

CHAPTER 6

To Worship in Spirit and in Truth

B eyond simply admitting Jesus into our hearts by believing and agreeing with His words (teachings), how do we ingest and operate in union with His Spirit? How do we function in this world operating out of His Spirit wisdom?

Many believe that just because they have confessed Christ they have the Holy Spirit. Others believe that because they pray in tongues they are Spirit-filled Christians. Although that may be the case, it takes something much more essential to operate in union with His Spirit. It requires obeying His Spirit and viewing life through the wisdom values of Jesus, and responding to life accordingly. Jesus sums up our spiritual duty and our New Covenant relationship with God through His encounter with the Samaritan woman at the well.

NIV Jn 4:19 *"Sir," the woman said, "I can see that you are a prophet.*
NIV Jn 4:20 *Our fathers worshiped on this mountain, but you Jews claim that the place where we must worship is in Jerusalem."*
NIV Jn 4:21 *Jesus declared, "Believe me, woman, a time is coming when you will worship the Father neither on this mountain nor in Jerusalem.*
NIV Jn 4:22 *You Samaritans worship what you do not know; we worship what we do know, for salvation is from the Jews.*
NIV Jn 4:23 *Yet a time is coming and has now come when the true worshipers will worship the Father in spirit and truth, for they are the kind of worshipers the Father seeks.*
NIV Jn 4:24 *God is spirit, and his worshipers must worship in spirit and in truth."*

If Jesus came here to do what it took for us to have a New Covenant relationship with God, and He is telling this woman that this is the future; this is the new way to honor and worship God; and also is basically saying that He is now busy recruiting people who will relate to God in this manner, well then, this becomes one of the most important verses in the New Testament. Ironically, who in the contemporary Church actually teaches us how to worship God in this manner? Who even teaches what exactly spirit is, and what truth is, meaning in respect to exactly which truth? And how do we worship God in truth? Let's go forward by looking at both of these aspects of the New Covenant relationship with God.

What does it mean to worship God in spirit?

First of all, what is spirit?

Previously we have touched on what spirit is. Let us look a little closer since it is the human spirit with its wisdom that became corrupted, and it is the Holy Spirit with His wisdom which is the cure for what afflicts us. Spirit is life principle, life/power/energy, and consciousness or awareness (a sense of self and one's environment). The attributes of spirit are power and energy, causing animation; it is the source or the fountain of inspiration and motivation. To be inspired is to be inspirited with power to perform and pursue a thing. Other attributes of spirit are feelings (feelings are attributes of the spirit, whereas emotions are attributes of the soul). The native language of spirit is not words. Words are the language of the soul or the mind. Pictures, feelings, and experiences/memories are the language of spirit.

Memory: The spirit holds all memories and the feelings of them. In psychology certain aspects of spirit are labeled as the subconscious mind—

that place beyond words where all the deep rooted memories, feelings, experiences, and traumas are stored.

The spirit is experiential. It understands things through experience. The mind or soul, on the other hand, can understand things with words and concepts. Wisdom is an attribute of the spirit, and intelligence is an attribute of the mind/soul. Spirit wisdom considers matters with experiential knowledge. The intelligence of the mind considers things through the use of words, and factors in the experiential wisdom that comes from the spirit after translating the spirit wisdom and spirit feelings into words. The mind can change through concepts and words, but the spirit changes through experience. It is most difficult to change the feelings of spirit by understanding things conceptually, especially when the spirit relies on or thinks with feelings, pictures, and memories.

For example, you were in a car accident and were traumatized with fear and pain. You can understand the concept that cars are safe and it is ok to ride in them again with your mind. However, in that place beyond words, the spirit (which gives consciousness to the mind) fills your mind with a consciousness charged with feelings of fear and apprehension. It causes overwhelming anxiety to flood your mind at the very thought of getting into a car. Most people dealing with this would consider themselves to have irrational fears because they know cars are safe and they want to ride in them so they don't understand their feelings. But spirit feelings of fear and anxiety overwhelm the mind and intelligence preventing that person from entering into the car. The three natures of the man are in conflict with each other, and he doesn't understand himself.

The spirit of a man can be in conflict with the soul or mind of the man. Again, the mind can reason and rationalize with concepts and words knowing that a ride in the car is safe. But to the man's spirit (that place in him which is beyond words), words and rationales' count for very little.

What counts is experience! " You can't tell me anything, I've been there, done that, and bought the tee-shirt. I've been in a car and almost got killed, they are not safe and they are something to fear!"

It is only through further experiences of riding in the car multiple times without getting in an accident or being harmed that the spirit of the man can finally feel (through that new experience) that it is ok to ride in a car and that they are safe. Now, through experience, the spirit of the man has caught up with the rational mind/soul of the man, and they are no longer in conflict.

This is why the concept of, "getting back in the saddle" after being thrown by a horse is so important. In the case of a car, it is found to be beneficial to, as soon as possible, get back in a car and experience riding after having been in a traumatic accident. This is so the fear of cars doesn't have time to settle in (your spirit).

Wisdom is of the spirit and knowledge is of the mind. This is why wisdom is sometimes defined as experiential knowledge. In other words, knowledge which has been attained through experience. As defined previously, wisdom is a set of values by which to perceive through. Not all wisdom is attained through experience. Originally, wisdom values started out as something our Creator endowed us with, like the software of a computer. Then, additional wisdom would be built upon that through the experiential knowledge of the man. However, as stated, the foundational wisdom values of the human spirit (Adam's spirit) endowed by God became corrupted by Adam ingesting the spirit of the Devil, as a result of seeking after a "different wisdom".

The spirit of the man will dictate a perceived awareness of something, without words, to the mind. Having that perceived awareness, the soul can understand a matter by translating and interpreting a description of that awareness with words. Then, processing those words through the intellect, emotions, the rationale, and the imagination, it understands a matter.

Attitude or outlook comes from the spirit perception, which fills the mind before it goes to work interpreting and assigning words to its spirit feelings. The perspective that the spirit sees matters from has a very powerful influence over the mind. The mind's understanding is limited by it. Just as a witness of an event that sees the event from one angle is limited in what he sees by that angle, another witness who sees it from a different angle can see the same event differently, making completely different observations and conclusions as a result. Both witnesses, intelligent as they may be, have limited understanding because of their perspective. The spirit perspective determines the light in which the mind understands everything.

The spirit's point of perspective is a product of the wisdom values of the spirit. As a result, if you have a downcast countenance and a negative spirit outlook or attitude, you will have negative thoughts and understandings of things. Conversely, if you have a positive spirit attitude, or outlook and perceive matters in a positive or enthusiastic light, the mind will understand matters in a positive and hopeful way.

The spirit gives life to both the mind and body of the man. The mind and the brain are two different things. The mind, in reality, is the soul of the man; whereas the physical brain primarily manages the body and its functions, as well as, translates and coordinates between the body, the soul/mind, and the spirit (which provides life-giving consciousness resulting in animations of the body and its functions).

Without spirit, both the body and the soul are dead. In the case of the soul, without spirit consciousness the mind is blind having no sense of anything—dead. In the same way, the brain is dead and has no sense of anything without both the life giving blood and the spirit energy impulses it receives through the nerves from the five awareness senses the body has (sight, sound, smell, taste, touch).

Likewise, the mind is alive and can function when filled with spirit life and consciousness/awareness. As stated before, the attributes of the mind, no matter how intelligent, are confined by the spirit's unique wisdom (perception and outlook) of what it is aware of, coupled with the inspired power (energy) springing forth from the spirit's motives.

Notwithstanding the dependency the soul has on the life-principle and consciousness of the spirit, the soul is superior to the spirit of the man. This is because the mind and will of the man are attributes of the soul and it directs the spirit power. Likewise, the Word or body of God and the Spirit of God are both subject to the mind and will of God (known to us as the Father). Father God is the same to God's triune being as the soul is to man's triune being. As it is said, we are made in His image. The Bible confirms the subordination of the spirit to the soul when it says:

^{Amp Pr 16:32} *He who is slow to anger is better than the mighty, he who rules his [own] spirit than he who takes a city.*

^{Amp Pr 25:28} *He who has no rule over his own spirit is like a city that is broken down and without walls.*

This person is defenseless, led by anything that comes along.

^{NLT Jas 1:6} *. . . as a wave of the sea that is driven and tossed by the wind.*

It is the same when it comes to the Holy Spirit (the disembodied Spirit of Christ) in us, He subjects Himself to our soul/mind and will. Otherwise, we would not have the capacity to obey His Spirit voluntarily as an act of love and union. Just as it says below in verse 32:

NIV 1Co 14:32 The spirits of prophets are subject to the control of prophets.

The motives, perception, and wisdom of a spirit are unique to the spirit. For example: The spirit of fear has a motive to control and suffers dread and anxiety when things go in a direction which it cannot control. It perceives things in a light of being in or out of its control.

The spirit of haughtiness has a motive of seeing itself as above all things and a judge of all things, knowing all. It perceives others in a light which elevates self by putting others down through finding fault and making judgments.

The Spirit of God, the Holy Spirit, has as its motive to serve and obey God. He desires to serve the heart, mind, and will of God, which we know as the Father. The Holy Spirit perceives things in light of how He can respond to, energize, make manifest, and empower the will of the Father. When we operate out of the Spirit of God, we too joyfully desire to spend our life on giving expression to the will of God (the Father) and not our own. We delight in living to obey Him—we are actually compelled to do so by the motives of the Holy Spirit within. That is why God gave us His Spirit as a part of His New Covenant promise when He said He will give us a Spirit which will cause us to obey Him.

As a final example:

The spirit of the Devil, which has been infused into the human spirit, has as his motives to be independent of God and to be god. This spirit sees things in light of a sense of entitlement which covets. As a result, it hates God, rebels against Him, and defies Him with a great hostility. Every root spirit that is evil is born out of the spirit of the Devil. Jesus said of the Devil that he was a liar from the beginning and is the father of all lies—false perceptions—which array themselves against the true knowledge of God (the true reality and nature of things).

Next question: Now that we know what spirit is, exactly how do we worship God in spirit?

Is praying in tongues the way to do it? Praying in tongues, if done out of the right spirit, certainly is a primal way to give free expression to the Holy Spirit while releasing His Spirit energy into the natural through our being. In this way, His cleansing Spirit washes through us. It also conditions us to disengage our own reasoning, intellect, and judgment, allowing these faculties to be inactive so that we can give expression to the Spirit unencumbered. This is why we speak out unintelligible words. It prohibits the mind from being involved, since we don't always know what we are speaking. Spirit power, feelings and will, have expression out of the body straight from the Spirit without the mind of the man involved or filtering these through his own understanding and sense of right and wrong.

If we are to be led by the Spirit, we must learn to set aside our own judgment and reasoning and be led directly by the Holy Spirit. However, we are meant to employ the faculties of the mind to discern if what we are picking up is the Spirit's will, and not our own. We then decide with the mind to give expression to the Holy Spirit, His will, and His promptings, or to give expression to our own will.

As beneficial and as edifying as it is, praying in tongues is only a small part of what Jesus meant when He said, God is looking for worshipers who will worship him in spirit. In fact, praying in tongues is almost rendered meaningless if we do not worship God in spirit the primary and foundational way the Bible teaches. The following verses sum up that primary or foundational way of how to worship God in spirit:

Amp Jn 14:15 *If you [really] love Me, you will keep (obey) My commands.*

Amp Jn 14:16 And I will ask the Father, and He will give you another Comforter *(Counselor, Helper, Intercessor, Advocate, Strengthener, and Standby), that He may remain with you forever—*

Amp Jn 14:17 The Spirit of Truth, Whom the world cannot receive (welcome, take to its heart), because it does not see Him or know and recognize Him. But you know and recognize Him, for He lives with you [constantly] and will be in you.*

Amp Jn 14:18 I will not leave you as orphans [comfortless, desolate, bereaved, forlorn, helpless]; I will come [back] to you.*

Amp Jn 14:19 Just a little while now, and the world will not see Me any more, but you will see Me; because I live, you will live also.*

Amp Jn 14:20 At that time [when that day comes] you will know [for yourselves] that I am in My Father, and you [are] in Me, and I [am] in you.*

Amp Jn 14:21 The person who has My commands and keeps them is the one who [really] loves Me; and whoever [really] loves Me will be loved by My Father, and I [too] will love him and will show (reveal, manifest) Myself to him. [I will let Myself be clearly seen by him and make Myself real to him.]*

Amp Jn 14:22 Judas, not Iscariot, asked Him, Lord, how is it that You will reveal Yourself [make Yourself real] to us and not to the world?*

Amp Jn 14:23 Jesus answered, If a person [really] loves Me, he will keep My word [obey My teaching]; and My Father will love him, and We will come to him and make Our home (abode, special dwelling place) with him.*

Amp Jn 14:24 Anyone who does not [really] love Me does not observe and obey My teaching. And the teaching which you hear and heed is not Mine, but [comes] from the Father Who sent Me.*

To worship God in spirit is to hearken (to listen, to give heed and respectful attention) to God's Spirit within, and obey every one of His promptings. In doing so, we fall into union with Him, and become one with Him.

Amp Ro 7:6 But now we are discharged from the Law and have terminated all intercourse with it, having died to what once restrained and held us captive. So* *now we serve not under [obedience to] the old code of written regulations, but [under obedience to the promptings] of the Spirit in newness [of life].*

When it says, "if you love me you will obey my commands," it has a far deeper meaning than just being a condition Jesus is putting on loving Him. He is not saying, "to prove you love me you must show me by obeying." Instead He is saying, "to obey me is to love me." This concept (if you can call it that) of showing your love for Him by obeying Him runs much deeper than merely showing loyalty and, through obedience, a demonstration of devotion. Instead, these words outline the entirety of the spiritual principle of union with Christ.

To love Jesus is to become intimately one with Him. How do we experience intimacy with God? How is it possible to be in a union with Christ and be one with Him as He is with His Father? Especially considering He is only in the earth as a disembodied Spirit. To become one with Christ is to be moved by His Spirit and not by one's own human spirit. As a result, His Spirit is the common denominator which makes us together with Christ one—two people in union reconciled as one whole person.

What exactly binds us to His Spirit so that we are one in union with Him? There is only one thing: to relate to Jesus as He related to His Father in Heaven. The binding straps which secure us to His Spirit are obedience. To be moved by His Spirit is to obey His Spirit, giving expression to Him with our life and not expression of our own will. Nothing else can make us in union, or one, with Jesus.

Like dancing together, moving in graceful unison, voluntarily obeying His Spirit promptings out of love (a desire to be one with Him) is the way in which we can tether ourselves to His Spirit, becoming one. It is the only way! The more we follow the lead of His Spirit promptings and carry them out in His rhythms and timing, the more perfect our dance with Him becomes, causing us both to move more perfectly as one. To love Jesus and to be more intimate with Him is to obey Him. There is no other way! To die to self in this way is to become alive in Christ. This is when we become His bride.

Jesus has expressed His love for us by dying to His body, yet remaining in the earth with His disembodied Spirit. We die to our life in the body by laying down our own agendas, desires, ambitions, and will. In doing so, we no longer live for ourselves, but express our love by living to be the embodiment of His disembodied Spirit in us. We then carry out in our body the will and promptings of Jesus as He compels and prompts us through His Spirit. He died to His body, we die to our life in the body. In doing so, we are no longer moved by the corrupt spirit we inherited from Adam. Instead, the two become one, living for each other, married in union.

Amp Jn 14:23 If a person [really] loves Me, he will keep My word [obey My teaching]; and My Father will love him, and We will come to him and make Our home (abode, special dwelling place) with him.

Amp Jn 14:20 At that time [when that day comes] you will know [for yourselves] that I am in My Father, and you [are] in Me, and I [am] in you.

To sum it up, being in union with Jesus is to voluntarily out of love and out of a desire to be one with Him, obey His Spirit. The more we hearken to His Spirit and obey His promptings, the more intimate and unified we become, connected with Him as one whole person. We experience life as one by doing His will. By experiencing the responses the world has to what we say or do, we experience the world's response to God. All the while they do not know that we are a new creation and the person they are looking at is dead to their own life, and Christ is living and speaking through them.

Amp Jn 14:15 *If you [really] love Me, you will keep (obey) My commands.*

Amp Jn 14:16 *And I will ask the Father, and He will give you another Comforter (Counselor, Helper, Intercessor, Advocate, Strengthener, and Standby), that He may remain with you forever—*

Amp Jn 14:17 *The Spirit of Truth, Whom the world cannot receive (welcome, take to its heart), because it does not see Him or know and recognize Him. But you know and recognize Him, for He lives with you [constantly] and will be in you.*

Amp Jn 14:22 *Judas, not Iscariot, asked Him, Lord, how is it that You will reveal Yourself [make Yourself real] to us and not to the world? ·*

Amp Jn 14:23 *Jesus answered, If a person [really] loves Me, he will keep My word [obey My teaching]; and My Father will love him, and We will come to him and make Our home (abode, special dwelling place) with him.*

Amp Jn 14:24 *Anyone who does not [really] love Me does not observe and obey My teaching. And the teaching which you hear and heed is not Mine, but [comes] from the Father Who sent Me.*

NIV Jn 13:20 *I tell you the truth, whoever accepts anyone I send accepts me; and whoever accepts me accepts the one who sent me."*

Amp Phil 3:10 *For my determined purpose is . . . that I may so share His sufferings as to be continually transformed [in spirit into His likeness even] to His death . . .*

This is not a task which we can sit back and let happen, or live life as we always have, waiting for the Lord to make Himself clear to us that He must be our first love above love for our own life. It requires not merely a passivity that when the Lord calls we will say yes, but a dogged devotion, and constant laying down of our own desires while searching out His. It is not an easy thing. It takes constant hard work for Paul tells us:

Amp 1Co 13:12 *For now we are looking in a mirror that gives only a dim (blurred) reflection [of reality as in a riddle or enigma], but then [when perfection comes] we shall see in reality and face to face! Now I know in part (imperfectly), but then I shall know and understand fully and clearly, even in the same manner as I have been fully and clearly known and understood [by God].*

And again David instructs us:

Amp Ps 131:1 LORD, MY heart is not haughty, nor my eyes lofty; neither do I exercise myself in matters too great or in things too wonderful for me.
Amp Ps 131:2 Surely I have calmed and quieted my soul; like a weaned child with his mother, like a weaned child is my soul within me [ceased from fretting].
Amp Ps 131:3 O Israel, hope in the Lord from this time forth and forever.

We must quiet our own passions and desires so that we may hear that still small voice, or have a sense of the direction the current that His Spirit is flowing in. We must use all reasoning and our entire faculties to know and properly interpret the Spirit promptings we sense in our hearts. We must sift through it all to know His will in a matter by weighing our intuitive gut feelings alongside our visions and dreams, the written Word, and agreement with others who have proven themselves in union with Christ. And finally we must employ an athlete's and soldier's discipline to wait upon the Lord and move only after we receive and interpret our marching orders, even when loss or danger is charging towards us.

As long as we walk this earth, we must have faith, be daring, and even risk it all while understanding Him through a blurred and, at times, vague clarity. However, His promise is this:

NIV Ro 4:3 What does the Scripture say? "Abraham believed God, and it was credited to him as righteousness."

NIV Ro 4:13 *It was not through law that Abraham and his offspring received the promise that he would be heir of the world, but through the righteousness that comes by faith.*

NIV Ro 8:28 *And we know that in all things God works for the good of those who love him, who have been called according to his purpose.*
NIV Ro 8:29 *For those God foreknew he also predestined to be conformed to the likeness of his Son, that he might be the firstborn among many brothers.*
NIV Ro 8:30 *And those he predestined, he also called; those he called, he also justified; those he justified, he also glorified.*
NIV Ro 8:31 *What, then, shall we say in response to this? If God is for us, who can be against us?*

We who risk it all, following the will of God as expressed through His Spirit and interpreted intuitively through our conscience, have a distinct advantage over those who act out of their own wisdom and desires. If they are wrong in their choices and offend the Lord, they are simply wrong and must suffer the consequences of their choices. However, because of our sincere heart to serve the will of the Lord and not our own will; for us who live by faith but happen to unwittingly miss the mark, the Lord counts it as righteousness. This is because our motives and intentions are to do His will. He makes our choices work for our good instead of letting them dictate consequences which will serve to harm us.

Amp Jn 7:18 *He who speaks on his own authority seeks to win honor for himself. [He whose teaching originates with himself seeks his own glory.] But He Who seeks the glory and is eager for the honor of Him Who sent Him, He is true; and there is no unrighteousness or falsehood or deception in Him.*

We are judged not by whether or not we make a right choice or wrong one, but by our motive and intent! This single but subtle difference escapes the majority of believers. They operate as if it is the right or wrongness of their choice God judges their heart by, and not their motive and intent to do as they believe God is instructing them. For those devoted to serving Him, He makes every single experience endured somehow serve our good and the forming of our perfection. All this applies to us when we believe Jesus and worship Him in spirit.

To not strive to hearken to His Spirit, even to ignore His Spirit within, or act independently from it, is to disconnect from Him. It is spiritual adultery to forsake your first love and to love yourself first. When it says, "first love" it does not mean Jesus was the first person you ever loved. Rather, it means you obey Him first and foremost, respond to Him first, hold Him as a first priority, serve His will first, fulfilling His interest over anyone else's, including and especially your own. To lose your first love is to go back to loving your own life and pursuing your own desires and ambitions in life—to love yourself first in preference and in priority. " . . . He who has found his life will lose it, he who has lost his life for My sake will find it."

NAS MT 10:37 *"He who loves father or mother more than Me is not worthy of Me; and he who loves son or daughter more than Me is not worthy of Me.*
NAS MT 10:38 *"And he who does not take his cross and follow after Me is not worthy of Me.*
NAS MT 10:39 *" He who has found his life will lose it, and he who has lost his life for My sake will find it.*
NAS MT 10:40 *"He who receives you receives Me, and he who receives Me receives Him who sent Me.*

NAS LK 14:26 *" If anyone comes to Me, and does not hate his own father and mother and wife and children and brothers and sisters, yes, and even his own life, he cannot be My disciple.*
NAS LK 14:27 *"Whoever does not carry his own cross and come after Me cannot be My disciple.*
NAS LK 14:28 *"For which one of you, when he wants to build a tower, does not first sit down and calculate the cost to see if he has enough to complete it?*

NAS LK 14:29 "*Otherwise, when he has laid a foundation and is not able to finish, all who observe it begin to ridicule him,*
NAS LK 14:30 *saying, 'This man began to build and was not able to finish.'*
NAS LK 14:31 "*Or what king, when he sets out to meet another king in battle, will not first sit down and consider whether he is strong enough with ten thousand men to encounter the one coming against him with twenty thousand?*
NAS LK 14:32 "*Or else, while the other is still far away, he sends a delegation and asks for terms of peace.*
NAS LK 14:33 "*So then, none of you can be My disciple who does not give up all his own possessions.*

NIV 2Co 5:14 *For Christ's love compels us, because we are convinced that one died for all, and therefore all died.*
NIV 2Co 5:15 *And he died for all, that those who live should no longer live for themselves but for him who died for them and was raised again.*
NIV 2Co 5:16 *So from now on we regard no one from a worldly point of view* (We no longer look at them and understand them according to the wisdom of this world). *Though we once regarded Christ in this way, we do so no longer.*
NIV 2Co 5:17 *Therefore, if anyone is in Christ, he is a new creation; the old has gone, the new has come!*
NIV 2Co 5:18 *All this is from God, who reconciled us to himself through Christ and gave us the ministry of reconciliation:*
NIV 2Co 5:19 *that God was reconciling the world to himself in Christ, not counting men's sins against them. And he has committed to us the message of reconciliation.*
NIV 2Co 5:20 *We are therefore Christ's ambassadors . . .*

This type of union is as Paul describes to the Galatians and to the Philippians:

NLT Gal 2:19 *For when I tried to keep the law, I realized I could never earn God's approval. So I died to the law so that I might live for God. I have been crucified with Christ.*

NLT Gal 2:20 *I myself no longer live, but Christ lives in me. So I live my life in this earthly body by trusting in the Son of God, who loved me and gave himself for me.*

NLT Gal 2:21 *I am not one of those who treats the grace of God as meaningless. For if we could be saved by keeping the law, then there was no need for Christ to die.*

Amp Phil 3:7 *But whatever former things I had that might have been gains to me, I have come to consider as [one combined] loss for Christ's sake.*

Amp Phil 3:8 *Yes, furthermore, I count everything as loss compared to the possession of the priceless privilege (the overwhelming preciousness, the surpassing worth, and supreme advantage) of knowing Christ Jesus my Lord and of progressively becoming more deeply and intimately acquainted with Him [of perceiving and recognizing and understanding Him more fully and clearly]. For His sake I have lost everything and consider it all to be mere rubbish (refuse, dregs), in order that I may win (gain) Christ (the Anointed One),*

Amp Phil 3:9 *And that I may [actually] be found and known as in Him, not having any [self-achieved] righteousness that can be called my own, based on my obedience to the Law's demands (ritualistic uprightness and supposed right standing with God thus acquired), but possessing that [genuine righteousness] which comes through faith in Christ (the Anointed One), the [truly] right standing with God, which comes from God by [saving] faith.*

Amp Phil 3:10 *[For my determined purpose is] that I may know Him [that I may progressively become more deeply and intimately acquainted with Him, perceiving and recognizing and understanding the wonders of His Person more strongly and more clearly], and that I may in that same way come to know the power outflowing from His resurrection [which it exerts over believers], and that I may so share His sufferings as to be continually transformed [in spirit into His likeness even] to His death, [in the hope]*

Amp Phil 3:11 *That if possible I may attain to the [spiritual and moral] resurrection [that lifts me] out from among the dead [even while in the body].*

Again, to worship God in spirit is to bind yourself to His Spirit. To be bound to His Spirit is to voluntarily, out of love and out of a desire to be one with Him, hearken to and obey His Spirit, causing the two to move in tandem and in union.

What does it mean to worship God in truth?

Does it mean we no longer lie or deceive and are honest about everything we say? Although that is the proper way to conduct ourselves, it is not what is meant here.

Amp Jn 18:37 *Pilate said to Him, Then You are a King? Jesus answered, You say it! [You speak correctly!] For I am a King. [Certainly I am a King!] This is why I was born, and for this I have come into the world, to bear witness to the Truth. Everyone who is of the Truth [who is a friend of the Truth, who belongs to the Truth] hears and listens to My voice.*
Amp Jn 18:38 *Pilate said to Him, What is Truth?*

Even though Jesus did not answer Pilate's question, all Christians should be asking this question, given that God is looking for worshipers who will worship Him in truth. Simply put, to worship God in truth is to worship God by perceiving and responding to our world through the wisdom values of Christ, and no longer out of the corrupt wisdom of the Devil. The wisdom of Christ is truth!

In other studies, we have taught what ingesting the fruit of the knowledge of good and evil was representative of. It was the ingesting of the wisdom values of the Devil, which forever and unrepairibly corrupted the perception and world view of man. He ingested the fruit because the serpent promised he would be like God. He did not become God, nor did he receive a power to be like God by ingesting the fruit. However, what did happen was Adam's spirit wisdom and perception—his world view— became a lie, and he then saw himself as if he were god, with him being the center of all things; with him as the beginning and end of all things:

self-sustaining, self-willed, self-serving, the judge of all things, with survival and desire dictating justice, right and wrong. The only thing that really changed was his perception of self. The wisdom of the spirit of the Devil is a lie!

The wisdom of the Devil are the values by which all humans since the fall perceive and understand their lives through. Although it is superficial, self-serving, unspiritual, evil, and from the Devil, it is our normal way of viewing our world. No matter how much we want to do good, with this world view, only bad will result. The human race may think themselves just, generous, good, and normal—just like everyone else—but the Lord said of our understanding:

NIV Ge 6:5 The LORD saw how great man's wickedness on the earth had become, and that every inclination of the thoughts of his heart was only evil all the time. NIV Ge 6:6 The LORD was grieved that he had made man on the earth, and his heart was filled with pain.

The lie is our entire worldview: our wisdom values which cause us to understand our world the way we do with our "me, myself and I" perception, making us gods from our own standpoint, even if we would never profess that we think we are god.

NIV Jn 1:17 For the law was given through Moses; grace and truth came through Jesus Christ.

James weighs our corrupt wisdom against the wisdom that comes from the Spirit of Christ in us. He verifies that the truth brought to us by Jesus is the wisdom which views all things as revolving around God and His will. He says of our own:

Amp Jas 3:14 But if you have bitter jealousy (envy) and contention (rivalry, selfish ambition) in your hearts, do not pride yourselves on it and thus be in defiance of and false to the Truth.

Amp Jas 3:15 This [superficial] wisdom is not such as comes down from above, but is earthly, unspiritual (animal), even devilish (demoniacal).

Amp Jas 3:16 For wherever there is jealousy (envy) and contention (rivalry and selfish ambition), there will also be confusion (unrest, disharmony, rebellion) and all sorts of evil and vile practices.

Paul admonishes his followers in the same way as James:

Amp 1Co 2:6 Yet when we are among the full-grown (spiritually mature Christians who are ripe in understanding), we do impart a [higher] wisdom (the knowledge of the divine plan previously hidden); but it is indeed not a wisdom of this present age or of this world nor of the leaders and rulers of this age, who are being brought to nothing and are doomed to pass away.

Amp 1Co 2:7 But rather what we are setting forth is a wisdom of God once hidden [from the human understanding] and now revealed to us by God—[that wisdom] which God devised and decreed before the ages for our glorification [to lift us into the glory of His presence].

Amp 1Co 2:8 None of the rulers of this age or world perceived and recognized and understood this, for if they had, they would never have crucified the Lord of glory.

Amp 1Co 3:3 For you are still [unspiritual, having the nature] of the flesh [under the control of ordinary impulses]. For as long as [there are] envying and jealousy and wrangling and factions among you, are you not unspiritual and of the flesh, behaving yourselves after a human standard and like mere (unchanged) men?

Amp Gal 5:15 But if you bite and devour one another [in partisan strife], be careful that you [and your whole fellowship] are not consumed by one another.

Amp Gal 5:17 For the desires of the flesh are opposed to the [Holy] Spirit, and the [desires of the] Spirit are opposed to the flesh (godless human nature); for these *are antagonistic to each other [continually withstanding and in conflict with each other], so that you are not free but are prevented from doing what you desire to do.*

Amp Gal 5:19 Now the doings (practices) of the flesh are clear (obvious): they are immorality, impurity, indecency,

Amp Gal 5:20 Idolatry, sorcery, enmity, strife, jealousy, anger (ill temper), selfishness, divisions (dissensions), party spirit (factions, sects with peculiar opinions, heresies),

Amp Gal 5:21 Envy, drunkenness, carousing, and the like. I warn you beforehand, just as I did previously, that those who do such things shall not inherit the kingdom of God.

When Paul says: "Now the doings (practices) of the flesh are clear (obvious) . . ." He is not talking about behavioral things that we should abstain from (although that is the case). However, his point is that if you operate out of the wisdom of this world and understand yourself in light of its perception (I, me, my) the result will be this bad fruit—these things will be the resulting practices of a person who perceives life out of the wisdom of this world. Again, he is not telling us to behave. Rather, he is educating us on the ensuing symptoms that occur when we perceive life out of the wisdom of this world.

Then James tells us about the wisdom we receive when we receive the Holy Spirit:

Amp Jas 3:17 But the wisdom from above is first of all pure (undefiled); then it is peace-loving, courteous (considerate, gentle). [It is willing to] yield to reason, full of compassion and good fruits; it is wholehearted and straightforward, impartial and unfeigned (free from doubts, wavering, and insincerity).

And again Paul:

NIV Ro 14:17 *For the kingdom of God is not a matter of eating and drinking, but of righteousness, peace and joy in the Holy Spirit,*
NIV Ro 14:18 *because anyone who serves Christ in this way is pleasing to God and approved by men.*
NIV Ro 14:19 *Let us therefore make every effort to do what leads to peace and to mutual edification.*

Amp Gal 5:16 *But I say, walk and live [habitually] in the [Holy] Spirit [responsive to and controlled and guided by the Spirit]; then you will certainly not gratify the cravings and desires of the flesh (of human nature without God).*
Amp Gal 5:18 *But if you are guided (led) by the [Holy] Spirit, you are not subject to the Law.*

When Paul says to habitually be responsive to and guided by the Holy Spirit, it is important to recognize that he is telling us we have to impose upon ourselves the habit of viewing our world out of the wisdom of Christ (the truth), and resist viewing our world according to the wisdom of the Devil. Since it is our default wisdom to view life out of our corrupt human spirit, it will take a concerted, focused and disciplined effort to view ourselves and our circumstances out of the wisdom of the Holy Spirit.

. . . we have a choice, a choice to enforce moment by moment!

Amp Gal 5:22 *But the fruit of the [Holy] Spirit [the work which His presence within accomplishes] is love, joy (gladness), peace, patience (an even temper, forbearance), kindness, goodness (benevolence), faithfulness,*
Amp Gal 5:23 *Gentleness (meekness, humility), self-control (self-restraint, continence). Against such things there is no law [that can bring a charge].*
Amp Gal 5:24 *And those who belong to Christ Jesus (the Messiah) have crucified the flesh (the godless human nature) with its passions and appetites and desires.*

Amp Gal 5:25 If we live by the [Holy] Spirit, let us also walk by the Spirit. [If by the Holy Spirit we have our life in God, let us go forward walking in line, our conduct controlled by the Spirit.]

Amp Gal 5:26 Let us not become vainglorious and self-conceited, competitive and challenging and provoking and irritating to one another, envying and being jealous of one another.

When Paul says, "the fruit of the Spirit," he means the fruit, or the ensuing product of operating out of the wisdom of the Spirit. The truth, which came through Jesus Christ, is the wisdom values (perception/worldview) endowed in His Spirit, which see God as the center, beginning, and end of all things. It gives us an identity as one in service to God and His will.

Amp Jas 3:17 But the wisdom from above is first of all pure (undefiled); then it is peace-loving, courteous (considerate, gentle). [It is willing to] yield to reason, full of compassion and good fruits; it is wholehearted and straightforward, impartial and unfeigned (free from doubts, wavering, and insincerity).

Amp Jas 3:18 And the harvest of righteousness (of conformity to God's will in thought and deed) is [the fruit of the seed] sown in peace by those who work for and make peace [in themselves and in others, that peace which means concord, agreement, and harmony between individuals, with undisturbedness, in a peaceful mind free from fears and agitating passions and moral conflicts].

Paul and James are not telling us that we should strive to have these kinds of mannerisms (although we should), but they are telling us to operate out of the wisdom of the Holy Spirit. They are saying that this should be the fruit or ensuing symptoms of someone who does. So what is very important to take note of here is that our focused efforts should not exclusively be applied towards having these mannerisms, but towards imposing upon ourselves to view our circumstances through the wisdom of the Holy Spirit. In doing so, these mannerisms will be the fruit of that discipline. We cannot stress enough that the goal is not to learn how to behave in a well mannered way, but the goal is to learn how to operate out of the wisdom of God which will result in the type of fruit that Paul and James are speaking to us about.

Continuing on, we hear Paul again (below) support exactly what James is saying (above):

NIV 1Co 1:30 It is because of him that you are in Christ Jesus, who has become for us wisdom from God—that is, our righteousness, holiness and redemption.
NIV 1Co 1:31 Therefore, as it is written: "Let him who boasts boast in the Lord."

Both James and Paul teach us that it is that simple; all they have to do is observe the fruit of our spiritual wisdom and then they can easily know by what wisdom values our world view perceives through. Either the wisdom that comes down from heaven, or worldly wisdom which is false to the truth, unspiritual, and of the Devil.

It's as simple as observing division, contention, jealousy and so on to know that we are operating out of the wrong spirit. That's all James and Paul needed to tell them. Unbelievable as it may seem, those ways of perceiving and interacting did not, and could not exist until the human spirit took on the wisdom of the Devil.

NIV 1Co 3:3 You are still worldly. For since there is jealousy and quarreling among you, are you not worldly? Are you not acting like mere men?

The people Paul is addressing in verse 3 above are not worshipping God in truth. They are not viewing each other out of the wisdom that comes down from heaven, but, instead, the wisdom of this world. To worship God in truth is to impose upon ourselves the worldview/wisdom of the Spirit of Christ within us. This is a discipline which requires total self-distrust and an abandonment of our own wisdom and understanding. If we so much as relax and consider things as we normally would, we will lose our grip and our world view will return to what it was. To worship God in truth, we must force ourselves to look upon life in a totally antagonistic way to our natural way. Out of consistent and vigilant efforts to do so, we will establish ourselves in a new spirit wisdom—the wisdom of Christ, and then His wisdom will eventually become our default worldview as long as we keep Him as our first love.

To worship the Lord in this way, by the power of His Spirit, is to correct within oneself all that was corrupted in the garden. In regards to worshiping God in spirit and in truth, to do one without the other is to fall short of perfect union with the Lord. It is to be confused, conflicted, and to do things begrudgingly or out of bitterness, and seeing the Lord as bondage forcing Himself and His will upon you.

It is important to recognize that since the first-century these verses and the rest of the New Testament have been understood in a worldly, superficial way. That is, they are understood as some kind of behavioral standard we must live by. As Paul admonished us:

NIV 1Co 3:1 Brothers, I could not address you as spiritual but as worldly—mere infants in Christ.
NIV 1Co 3:2 I gave you milk, not solid food, for you were not yet ready for it. Indeed, you are still not ready.

However, if we were to understand the sample of verses shown above in a spiritual sense, we would understand they are not talking about conducting ourselves behaviorally, but about helping us understand by which wisdom we should operate out of so that our world view is such that the fruit of it is reflected in our conduct and lines up with what they describe.

The Apostles, including James and Paul, knew from the beginning what has since been lost; it is the Spirit of Christ with His power and His wisdom/world view that has the only chance to overcome the defect in man produced by having ingested the power and wisdom of the Devil, by Adam, into the human spirit. If we don't make our focus living and viewing our world in the ways of the wisdom of Jesus then the teachings of the New Testament cannot help us. Paul foresees and warns us about not worshiping God in truth (living by the wisdom of heaven):

Amp 2Ti 3:1 *BUT UNDERSTAND this, that in the last days will come (set in) perilous times of great stress and trouble [hard to deal with and hard to bear].*
Amp 2Ti 3:2 *For people will be lovers of self and [utterly] self-centered, lovers of money and aroused by an inordinate [greedy] desire for wealth, proud and arrogant and contemptuous boasters. They will be abusive (blasphemous, scoffing), disobedient to parents, ungrateful, unholy and profane.*
Amp 2Ti 3:3 *[They will be] without natural [human] affection (callous and inhuman), relentless (admitting of no truce or appeasement); [they will be] slanderers (false accusers, troublemakers), intemperate and loose in morals and conduct, uncontrolled and fierce, haters of good.*
Amp 2Ti 3:4 *[They will be] treacherous [betrayers], rash, [and] inflated with self-conceit. [They will be] lovers of sensual pleasures and vain amusements more than and rather than lovers of God.*
Amp 2Ti 3:5 *For [although] they hold a form of piety (true religion), they deny and reject and are strangers to the power of it [their conduct belies the genuineness of their profession]. Avoid [all] such people [turn away from them].*

Remembering what James spoke about the two wisdoms, it is the worldly wisdom from the Devil which produces the kind of world view Paul speaks of to Timothy (above).

NIV Jas 3:13 *Who is wise and understanding among you? Let him show it by his good life, by deeds done in the humility that comes from wisdom.*
NIV Jas 3:14 *But if you harbor bitter envy and selfish ambition in your hearts, do not boast about it or deny the truth.*

NIV Jas 3:15 *Such "wisdom" does not come down from heaven but is earthly, unspiritual, of the devil.*

NIV Jas 3:16 *For where you have envy and selfish ambition, there you find disorder and every evil practice.*

NIV Jas 3:17 *But the wisdom that comes from heaven is first of all pure; then peace-loving, considerate, submissive, full of mercy and good fruit, impartial and sincere.*

NIV Jas 3:18 *Peacemakers who sow in peace raise a harvest of righteousness.*

It is by no magic that Paul knew that people would perceive life with the attitude he outlined for Timothy. Even Jesus told us in the Gospel of Matthew and in Revelation that this would be the case. Even the Church has stopped operating out of the wisdom from Heaven Jesus died to give them.

NIV Mt 24:10 *At that time many will turn away from the faith and will betray and hate each other,*

NIV Mt 24:11 *and many false prophets will appear and deceive many people.*

NIV Mt 24:12 *Because of the increase of wickedness, the love of most will grow cold,*

NIV Mt 24:13 *but he who stands firm to the end will be saved.*

NIV Rev 2:4 *Yet I hold this against you: You have forsaken your first love.*

NIV Rev 2:5 *Remember the height from which you have fallen! Repent and do the things you did at first. If you do not repent, I will come to you and remove your lampstand from its place.*

When we hold Jesus as our first love (first in priority and preference), it is at the expense of forsaking our own life as our first love. In doing so, we operate out of the wisdom that the Spirit of Christ has. When we love ourselves first in priority and preference, we operate out of our own sinful spirit and its wisdom. What Paul and Jesus warns us about—losing the understanding and the true power of His Spirit to overcome the human defect—has been the case, even since the end of the first-century.

In almost all of Paul's letters, which are recorded in the Bible, he combats the loss of pursuing true wisdom and the Spirit's power to overcome the human defect—the forsaking of our first love.

Ever since the Reformation began in the 1500's, the Christian Church has been trying to recapture true understanding of the gift Jesus died to give us. However, centuries later, even to this day (notwithstanding the contemporary movement to be Spirit-filled), the power of enlightened wisdom has still not been recovered by the Church as a whole. We are in the times Paul told Timothy was to come.

CHAPTER 7

The Beatitudes

T he law given by Moses can be summarized by the Ten Commandments. The teachings of Jesus can be summarized by the Sermon on the Mount.

How do we know what it looks like to operate out of heavenly wisdom? What are the righteous (or spiritual) requirements of the law? How do we follow them in a way that is not just outwardly if we don't know how or what they are? Do we only have what the Apostles wrote as admonishments to help us realize after it's too late that we are operating out of the wisdom of this world? We must have more than to simply pray out loud unintelligible words we don't understand so that we know we are within the principles of the spirit realm.

Jesus' teachings tell us how. Jesus addresses the same issues in His teachings that the law of Moses did. There is, however, an important distinction between the law that Moses gave us and the teachings Jesus gave us. The distinction does not change the law of Moses, nor does it raise the standard in a stricter way. Jesus teaches us the boundaries of the same laws that achieve a spiritual conformity (the righteous requirements of the law).

It says that the light came into the world. By Jesus giving us His Spirit which gives us spiritual sight, a power to conform, and teachings that conform to the principles of the spirit realm, He is bringing enlightenment into the world on a massive scale. He is giving us an enlightenment no teacher on earth can equal. Even the greatest sages, philosophers, and gurus ever to have walked the face of the earth are spiritually blind to the truth. Now that He has come, He tells us to leave our parents, teachers, leaders, even our own lives behind. They all are (spiritually) blind guides. To His followers, He admonishes them concerning His enlightenment compared to theirs:

NIV Mt 15:14 . . . *Leave them; they are blind guides. If a blind man leads a blind man, both will fall into a pit."*

Now that His enlightenment is finally here, He admonishes the teachers and leaders by saying:

NLT Mt 23:8 *Don't ever let anyone call you 'Rabbi,' for you have only one teacher, and all of you are on the same level as brothers and sisters.*
NLT Mt 23:9 *And don't address anyone here on earth as 'Father,' for only God in heaven is your spiritual Father.*
NLT Mt 23:10 *And don't let anyone call you 'Master,' for there is only one master, the Messiah.*
NLT Mt 23:11 *The greatest among you must be a servant.*
NLT Mt 23:12 *But those who exalt themselves will be humbled, and those who humble themselves will be exalted.*

Jesus' teachings are spiritual laws and principles that spiritual men and women must live by since their true domain has become the spiritual realm, even while in the body. However, they are soon to have a celestial body for their soul and, thereafter, reside fully in the spiritual realm.

It is, however, common to think of the distinction between Him and Moses as Jesus raising the bar or kicking it up a notch. For example, Moses' law says do not commit adultery. Jesus seemingly makes the same law stricter by saying, "if you even look upon a woman lustfully you have committed adultery in your heart." It is not the case that He is making the law of Moses stricter. What truly distinguishes the law of Moses and Jesus' teachings from each other is that Moses is more descriptive of the behavioral aspect (although Paul tells us that the true nature of the law is spiritual). Jesus, on the other hand, focused on and taught us the spiritual aspect of the same law.

We know what boundaries not to cross in our behavior through Moses. Jesus spent little time teaching us that in the Bible. Instead, the focus of His teachings was the boundaries of where we should not let our desires, imagination, thoughts and spirit feelings go. By doing so, Jesus made the spirit realm not only real, but pertinent, even the primary state we as men should conform to.

Most God fearing people discipline themselves in a way in which (relatively speaking) they restrain themselves from acting on most of the feelings and desires they have in their heart that are sinful. However, the same people have a decided lack of discipline when it comes to preventing their hearts from crossing the same boundaries with their feelings and desires. Being unspiritual, they think that doesn't really count. In their reasoning, it's only what they do or don't do that really counts. In fact, it is common for them to think that they can't help what they feel. As such, they allow their hearts to be tantalized with the feeling of exploring the lust, anger, or jealousy they think they can't help but feel, but would never act on.

"I can't help it, it's just the way I feel!" It is an unspiritual and a ridiculous notion that you can stop your flesh from doing sinful things, but cannot help where you let your (spirit) feelings go. If with our minds we can stop our flesh from acting out, then with our minds we can stop ourselves from harboring or exploring sinful feelings and notions.

By the laws of Moses, we learn how to conduct ourselves behaviorally, and by the teachings of Jesus, we learn how to conduct ourselves spiritually. By Moses' laws we know boundaries of behavior, and by Jesus' teachings we know spiritual boundaries. The defect in man is completely wrapped up in our inability to know spiritual boundaries or the importance of adhering to them in our hearts. Jesus came to give spiritual boundaries, sight, and the power we need to become spiritual men and women and, thus, overcome our defect.

Furthermore, Jesus tried to help us understand that He is not changing the law or canceling it out by His teachings, but rather, through His teachings of the spiritual aspect of them (the righteous requirements of them), He is actually fulfilling them in every aspect. He is doing what the law of Moses could not do. Better said, He is obeying the law holistically, both spiritually and behaviorally. And in doing so, He is bringing into perfect execution and utter completion the promises, judgments, plans and words of God as He promised in Jeremiah 31:35. After all, being the Word of God Himself, He is the actual and perfectly precise manifestation of the words God speaks.

NIV Mt 5:17 "_Do not think that I have come to abolish the Law or the Prophets; I have not come to abolish them but to fulfill them._

NIV Mt 5:18 _I tell you the truth, until heaven and earth disappear, not the smallest letter, not the least stroke of a pen, will by any means disappear from the Law until everything is accomplished._

NIV Mt 5:19 _Anyone who breaks one of the least of these commandments and teaches others to do the same will be called least in the kingdom of heaven, but whoever practices and teaches these commands will be called great in the kingdom of heaven._

NIV Mt 5:20 _For I tell you that unless your righteousness surpasses that of the Pharisees and the teachers of the law_ (who were superficial and unspiritual in their leadership, teachings, and personal lives), _you will certainly not enter the kingdom of heaven._

In order to bring into perfect fulfillment the law and the promises made through the prophets, there must be spiritual conformity both in the heart and in our outward conformity. As my mother would say when she would force us to do something and we would continually object to it, "You are going to do it and like it!" In an overly simplistic way Moses is addressing the "do it" part my mother speaks of, and Jesus the "like it" part.

If one day we are to be celestial humans and have our natural habitat in the spirit realm, we need to learn how to live by the "righteous (spiritual) requirements of the law." We need to learn to not just keep the law outwardly, but also in the invisible nature of our hearts. If, by the power of His Spirit within us, we keep His teachings, Jesus promises us:

Amp Jn 8:51 I assure you, most solemnly I tell you, if anyone observes My teaching [lives in accordance with My message, keeps My word], he will by no means ever see and experience death.

Amp Jn 5:24 I assure you, most solemnly I tell you, the person whose ears are open to My words [who listens to My message] and believes and trusts in and clings to and relies on Him Who sent Me has (possesses now) eternal life. And he does not come into judgment [does not incur sentence of judgment, will not come under condemnation], but he has already passed over out of death into life.

This statement does sound perplexing considering that since Jesus' work on the cross there is no Christian who has not died to his body. However, the Lord knows people live on when they die (as we call it). They become a disembodied soul. He does not consider death the end of life, but a state of nakedness; a state in which the invisible soul is unclothed with either a physical or spiritual body.

The way His promise becomes true is that if we keep His teachings, that is to worship God in spirit and in truth, we will never die and become a disembodied soul (unclothed and naked), even for a fraction of a second. We will not taste death at all! Like Stephen (the first martyr and follower of Christ to die after the cross), whoever is in union with Christ will, in the blink of an eye, be clothed in a new celestial body, standing before the Lord in heaven even before the head of his physical body hits the ground in death. He will not be there in his physical body, even during the last few breaths it draws during the pangs of death. His body will be like the proverbial chicken with his head cut off, animated by the last of the life force and blood left in the body. However, the real man will be before the throne, clothed in the splendor of a celestial body.

This is something which has to happen! The Christ follower in union with Jesus at one point or another, must exchange his physical body for a celestial body, never being caught naked while doing so. Again, the Lord's promise is that even before our physical body dies, we will be gone, clothed in a celestial body, and, therefore, we will not experience death. Jesus' words are made true!

NIV 1Co 15:55 *O death, where is your victory? O death, where is your sting?*

Death, you took away my physical body, but before you had a chance to do that I was clothed in a better body—so your efforts were in vain, you have no victory, and you have gained nothing in me, nor did you sting me by causing me to be disembodied. In this way, it is literal that Jesus died for us. He experienced death—to become disembodied. He then remained in the world as a disembodied Spirit so that we could be one, His Spirit in union with us having expression through our body. He did this so that we would never have to experience death in any form, as He had, but be clothed with a spiritual body before our head even hits the ground in death. Alive, forever! That is His promise and His sacrifice for us who are in a New Covenant relationship with Jesus. It is important to recognize, as Jesus told us, alive forever does not start when we die. Rather, it has already started and we will never die, even though we will exchange what our soul is clothed with. Even that is done to upgrade us from a physical body to a celestial body with no death (or disembodiment) involved. In this sense, we will never be caught naked.

We will now look at the spiritual requirements of the law, as taught by Jesus, and their implications on our lives and hearts. While reading these, keep in mind that Jesus' teachings are not upgrading, replacing, changing, or negating the laws given by Moses. However, by obeying His teachings, and by the power of His Spirit to do so, we will overcome the defect that dooms all humans to destruction. We will do this primarily using the Sermon on the Mount.

Amp Mt 15:1 THEN FROM Jerusalem came scribes and Pharisees and said,

Amp Mt 15:2 Why do Your disciples transgress and violate the rules handed down by the elders of the past? For they do not practice [ceremonially] washing their hands before they eat.

Amp Mt 15:3 He replied to them, And why also do you transgress and violate the commandment of God for the sake of the rules handed down to you by your forefathers (the elders)?

Amp Mt 15:4 For God commanded, Honor your father and your mother, and, He who curses or reviles or speaks evil of or abuses or treats improperly his father or mother, let him surely come to his end by death.

Amp Mt 15:5 But you say, If anyone tells his father or mother, What you would have gained from me [that is, the money and whatever I have that might be used for helping you] is already dedicated as a gift to God, then he is exempt and no longer under obligation to honor and help his father or his mother.

Amp Mt 15:6 So for the sake of your tradition (the rules handed down by your forefathers), you have set aside the Word of God [depriving it of force and authority and making it of no effect].

Amp Mt 15:7 You pretenders (hypocrites)! Admirably and truly did Isaiah prophesy of you when he said:

Amp Mt 15:8 These people draw near Me with their mouths and honor Me with their lips, but their hearts hold off and are far away from Me.

Amp Mt 15:9 *Uselessly do they worship Me, for they teach as doctrines the commands of men.*

Amp Mt 15:10 *And Jesus called the people to Him and said to them, Listen and grasp and comprehend this:*

Amp Mt 15:11 *It is not what goes into the mouth of a man that makes him unclean and defiled, but what comes out of the mouth; this makes a man unclean and defiles [him].*

Amp Mt 15:12 *Then the disciples came and said to Him, Do You know that the Pharisees were displeased and offended and indignant when they heard this saying?*

Amp Mt 15:13 *He answered, Every plant which My heavenly Father has not planted will be torn up by the roots.*

Amp Mt 15:14 *Let them alone and disregard them; they are blind guides and teachers. And if a blind man leads a blind man, both will fall into a ditch.*

Amp Mt 15:15 *But Peter said to Him, Explain this proverb (this maxim) to us.*

Amp Mt 15:16 *And He said, Are you also even yet dull and ignorant [without understanding and unable to put things together]?*

Amp Mt 15:17 *Do you not see and understand that whatever goes into the mouth passes into the abdomen and so passes on into the place where discharges are deposited?*

Amp Mt 15:18 *But whatever comes out of the mouth comes from the heart, and this is what makes a man unclean and defiles [him].*

Amp Mt 15:19 *For out of the heart come evil thoughts (reasonings and disputings and designs) such as murder, adultery, sexual vice, theft, false witnessing, slander, and irreverent speech.*

Amp Mt 15:20 *These are what make a man unclean and defile [him]; but eating with unwashed hands does not make him unclean or defile [him].*

The law Jesus confronted them about was called "Corban." The name of the treasury of the temple was called Corban, and the law was named after it. This is a classic example of using the law with ulterior motives— to look righteous as if serving God, but more often than not, use it to serve self-interest. By declaring Corban, one could look deeply spiritual because he was committing all his resources to the temple of God. Declaring this meant that any obligation one had for family, including support for one's own retired parents, was superseded, and no longer an obligation. According to the law, the resources of the person declaring Corban were now promised to the temple treasury.

Here's the catch. Family obligations were ongoing, according to the needs of one's family. A percentage of one's ongoing income was spent on the needs of others, making them unavailable for personal use. However, under Corban, you could give a lump sum donation hours before your death and avoid giving up a percentage of your ongoing income to family, allowing more cash flow for personal use. In this way you could use all of your income on yourself and give what you have at the end of your life to the temple; seeming to be a righteous and godly person in the eyes of men.

Thus Jesus calls them hypocrites. From a spiritual aspect, the defect in man prevents him from serving God in his heart, instead using the law to serve self. Jesus also instructed:

NIV Mt 6:24 *"No one can serve two masters. Either he will hate the one and love the other, or he will be devoted to the one and despise the other. You cannot serve both God and Money.*

Finally, in verses 18-20, Jesus makes it clear that the sinful motives and expressions of the heart (the spirit essence), are what defile a man, making him (spiritually) unclean. It is the sinful nature inherited in our human spirit that corrupts the soul and life in the body of an individual. It is from giving expression to his sinful spirit essence which corrupts every other nature of man (body and soul). "But whatever comes out of the mouth comes from the heart, and this is what makes a man unclean and defiles [him]. For out of the heart come evil thoughts (reasonings and disputings and designs) such as murder, adultery, sexual vice, theft, false witnessing, slander, and irreverent speech. These are what make a man unclean and defile [him] ... "

In other words, Jesus is teaching that the spirit essence is where the real problem exists—where something is in need of being made clean. It is not the body. Sin first comes from the outlook, motives, and intent (wisdom) of the spirit of man. When given expression, it corrupts and defiles the soul and body of the man. It is not the other way around.

NIV Mt 7:18 *A good tree cannot bear bad fruit, and a bad tree cannot bear good fruit.*

Jesus says a bad tree cannot bear good fruit. However, even more remarkable, is that a good tree cannot bear bad fruit. This is a direct reference to the two trees in the garden—the tree of life and the tree of the knowledge of good and evil. Fruit can only be in keeping with the quality of the Spirit it came from. Jesus is saying the same thing here as when He taught you cannot serve two masters, and Paul taught whatever rules you, you are a slave to. A bad tree cannot bear good fruit.

Moses wasn't allowed to enter the Promised Land because he struck the rock that produced water for the thirsty Israelites. God had instructed him to speak to the rock, not strike it. At face value, this might seem a harsh consequence for all of the good Moses did on God's behalf.

If we look at it closer, we will find out that Moses may have been unnerved by all of the threats against him and frustrated by all of the complaints. These people as much as attacked Moses, blaming him and taking their fears out on him because of their lack of water. Moses did as the Lord requested and performed the miracle which brought them water out of a rock. However, Moses' obedience to perform the miracle asked of him didn't serve or represent the Lord's intent for providing the water. He used this task of producing water from a rock in order to serve his own feelings and concerns. He struck the rock out of anger. Like, "here's your stinkin water, now get off my back!" Moses used the miracle to give expression to his anger over the people. The miracle served to shame the Israelites for blaming Moses. However, God requested he do the miracle to give expression to His compassion for people, setting them free from their fears. The good Moses did, did not serve the good it was intended to serve. Instead it served the bad feelings and frustrations Moses had towards these stiff necked people.

This is because if your master is sin, then whatever you do, good or bad, right or wrong, will serve the sin in you and not the good you want to serve. Conversely, a good tree cannot bear bad fruit. If God is our master, whatever we do serves good when we serve Him. This is why John says so plainly:

Amp 1Jn 3:8 *[But] he who commits sin [who practices evildoing] is of the devil [takes his character from the evil one], for the devil has sinned (violated the divine law) from the beginning. The reason the Son of God was made manifest (visible) was to undo (destroy, loosen, and dissolve) the works the devil [has done].*

Amp 1Jn 3:9 *No one born (begotten) of God [deliberately, knowingly, and habitually] practices sin, for God's nature abides in him [His principle of life, the divine sperm, remains permanently within him]; and he cannot practice sinning because he is born (begotten) of God.*

Amp 1Jn 3:10 *By this it is made clear who take their nature from God and are His children and who take their nature from the devil and are his children: no one who does not practice righteousness [who does not conform to God's will in purpose, thought, and action] is of God; neither is anyone who does not love his brother (his fellow believer in Christ).*

However, all men are born with the corrupted human spirit. That is, all except one, Jesus, who was born with the uncorrupted Spirit of God. By His Spirit, we can produce good fruit.

NIV Ge 4:6 Then the LORD said to Cain, "Why are you angry? Why is your face downcast?

NIV Ge 4:7 If you do what is right, will you not be accepted? But if you do not do what is right, sin is crouching at your door; it desires to have you, but you must master it.

And again, it is the mastering and the keeping of these evil tendencies of the spirit in check which keeps us from corrupting and defiling the soul and body. Conversely, not doing so causes us to give ourselves over to the bondage and service of the sin within. However, since you cannot get good fruit from a bad tree (our human spirit), it is by the Spirit of Christ (the good tree) in us that we can have the power to keep in check the evil tendencies of our sin nature, and likewise, bear good fruit, from His good Spirit, whose motive is to serve God and not self.

Amp Jas 4:4 You [are like] unfaithful wives [having illicit love affairs with the world and breaking your marriage vow to God]! Do you not know that being the world's friend is being God's enemy? So whoever chooses to be a friend of the world takes his stand as an enemy of God.

Amp Jas 4:5 Or do you suppose that the Scripture is speaking to no purpose that says, The Spirit Whom He has caused to dwell in us yearns over us and He yearns for the Spirit [to be welcome] with a jealous love?

Amp Jas 4:6 But He gives us more and more grace (power of the Holy Spirit, to meet this evil tendency and all others fully). That is why He says, God sets Himself against the proud and haughty, but gives grace [continually] to the lowly (those who are humble enough to receive it).

Amp Jas 4:7 So be subject to God. Resist the devil [stand firm against him], and he will flee from you.

Amp Jas 4:8 Come close to God and He will come close to you. [Recognize that you are] sinners, get your soiled hands clean; [realize that you have been disloyal] wavering individuals with divided interests, and purify your hearts [of your spiritual adultery].

Amp Jas 4:9 *[As you draw near to God] be deeply penitent and grieve, even weep [over your disloyalty]. Let your laughter be turned to grief and your mirth to dejection and heartfelt shame [for your sins].*

Amp Jas 4:10 *Humble yourselves [feeling very insignificant] in the presence of the Lord, and He will exalt you [He will lift you up and make your lives significant].*

The Sermon on the Mount:

NIV Mt 5:1 *Now when he saw the crowds, he went up on a mountainside and sat down. His disciples came to him,*

NIV Mt 5:2 *and he began to teach them, saying:*

NIV Mt 5:3 *"Blessed are the poor in spirit, for theirs is the kingdom of heaven.*

When He says, "poor in spirit" He is referring to individuals who do not have a strong, willful, self-empowering, and self-agitated spirit. It is only with a still and quiet spirit that man can hear God or have a sense of Him within himself. Only a passive and non-powerful spirit can fear God by yielding his will to that of God's. It was because of Paul's inability to rise up in spirit feelings and power (being poor in personal power) that he confessed he would come to the Corinthians in weakness, fear, and trembling. When they opposed him, or argued their case with him, they were agitated with personal spirit feelings and power/passions about what they thought was right and wrong.

It is typical that when we face others who stir up their spirit with passions and forcefulness, we normally rise up within our own spirit to match their power level. When we do, we are not intimidated by their expression of power. We become as adamant and passionate concerning our personal convictions as they. However, Paul, being poor in spirit, like a child, cannot rise up to the same level of passion and forcefulness as those he confronts with the truth. As such, like a child, their spirit power is overwhelming to him. Due to his "poor spirit," he is overwhelmed and brought into a state of weakness, fear, and trembling before their worldly, forceful, agitated spirit feelings and expression.

Amp 1Co 2:1 AS FOR *myself, brethren, when I came to you, I did not come proclaiming to you the testimony and evidence or mystery and secret of God [concerning what He has done through Christ for the salvation of men] in lofty words of eloquence or human philosophy and wisdom;*

Amp 1Co 2:2 For I resolved to know nothing (to be acquainted with nothing, to make a display of the knowledge of nothing, and to be conscious of nothing) among you except Jesus Christ (the Messiah) and Him crucified.

Amp 1Co 2:3 And I was in (passed into a state of) weakness and fear (dread) and great trembling [after I had come] among you.

Amp 1Co 2:4 And my language and my message were not set forth in persuasive (enticing and plausible) words of wisdom, but they were in demonstration of the [Holy] Spirit and power [a proof by the Spirit and power of God, operating on me and stirring in the minds of my hearers the most holy emotions and thus persuading them],

NIV 1Co 2:5 so that your faith might not rest on men's wisdom, but on God's power.

We can relate to Paul's condition with this example: Say there was a gathering at the home of a family, and people were laughing, excited, and having lively debate, in general a good time. Then suddenly a child got out of his bed and walked into the room. If one was to greet that child he would lower his voice and change his laughter to a disarming smile. He would bend down, completely lowering his energy level, and talk softly, making the child feel safe. Why? Because the energy level of the adult interaction is overwhelming to the child. It would frighten him and may cause him to cry. The child's spirit has not yet matured enough to handle the powerful and passionate strong feelings of an adult. Paul had passed into this childlike state. He was poor in spirit, or in a quieted and peaceful state. This being the case, he indeed experienced fear and trembling in his body when confronting worldly people with truth.

Paul, however, would not have it any other way. He had realized the meaning of the sayings of Jesus. Paul would boast that when he was weak, he was strong (in the Lord's Spirit). The Lord's Spirit would meet no resistance from Paul's human spirit when having expression through Paul, only because his spirit was so poor or weak that it was unable to oppose the expression of the Holy Spirit.

Amp 2Co 12:9 But He said to me, My grace (My favor and loving-kindness and mercy) is enough for you [sufficient against any danger and enables you to bear the trouble manfully]; for My strength and power are made perfect (fulfilled and completed) and show themselves most effective in [your] weakness. Therefore, I will all the more gladly glory in my weaknesses and infirmities, that the strength and power of Christ (the Messiah) may rest (yes, may pitch a tent over and dwell) upon me!
Amp 2Co 12:10 So for the sake of Christ, I am well pleased and take pleasure in infirmities, insults, hardships, persecutions, perplexities and distresses; for when I am weak [in human strength], then am I [truly] strong (able, powerful in divine strength).

NIV Ps 131:1 My heart is not proud, O LORD, my eyes are not haughty; I do not concern myself with great matters or things too wonderful for me.
NIV Ps 131:2 But I have stilled and quieted my soul; like a weaned child with its mother, like a weaned child is my soul within me.
NIV Ps 131:3 O Israel, put your hope in the LORD both now and forevermore.

Both David (Ps 131) and Paul understood the spiritual principle Jesus was teaching with this saying in verse 3; the poor, powerless, or quiet in spirit will have the Kingdom of Heaven.

NIV Mt 5:4 Blessed are those who mourn, for they will be comforted.
NIV Mt 5:5 Blessed are the meek, for they will inherit the earth.

Meekness, in the spiritual sense that Jesus was using it, is in line with being poor in spirit. Here is the Merriam-Webster definition of the word meek:

Meek:
Simple definition: Having or showing a quiet and gentle nature: not wanting to fight or argue with other people
1. enduring injury with patience and without resentment
2. deficient in spirit and courage
3. non-violent or strong[2]

Take note that the second definition is to be deficient or poor in spirit.

Two Biblical characters who were genuinely meek were David and Jesus. However, by their accounts they seemed to be anything but meek. Although they were fierce defenders of the honor of the Lord and His people, what made them meek, in the spiritual sense, was that they would not lift a finger to defend themselves. They relied solely on the Lord for His protection and justice. They both lived out the Scripture which said:

NAS DT 32:35 *'Vengeance is Mine, and retribution, In due time their foot will slip; For the day of their calamity is near, And the impending things are hastening upon them.'*

Jesus and David both clearly demonstrated their fierce determination to defend the honor of the Lord. For example: Jesus did so by clearing the temple of the activities which commercialized and profaned the worship of God, making it about money and profit. David did so by coming up against the giant Goliath when he profaned the name of the Lord and rendered the armies of Israel frozen with fear.

In defining meek some synonyms are: submissive, yielding, obedient, humble, timid, unprotesting, unresisting, like a lamb to slaughter.

Jesus indeed showed His meekness by being "The Lamb" led to slaughter. He was all of the synonyms listed above while being led off. In the case of David and because of his exploits as king, warrior and defender of Israel, it would be hard to see his meekness at face value. However, there is no question that is the case if one reads about him in the Bible. Here are a couple of examples of David's meekness:

NIV 2Sa 16:5 As King David approached Bahurim, a man from the same clan as Saul's family came out from there. His name was Shimei son of Gera, and he cursed as he came out.

NIV 2Sa 16:6 He pelted David and all the king's officials with stones, though all the troops and the special guard were on David's right and left.

NIV 2Sa 16:7 As he cursed, Shimei said, "Get out, get out, you man of blood, you scoundrel!

NIV 2Sa 16:8 The LORD has repaid you for all the blood you shed in the household of Saul, in whose place you have reigned. The LORD has handed the kingdom over to your son Absalom. You have come to ruin because you are a man of blood!"

NIV 2Sa 16:9 Then Abishai son of Zeruiah said to the king, "Why should this dead dog curse my lord the king? Let me go over and cut off his head."

NIV 2Sa 16:10 But the king said, "What do you and I have in common, you sons of Zeruiah? If he is cursing because the LORD said to him, 'Curse David,' who can ask, 'Why do you do this?' "

NIV 2Sa 16:11 David then said to Abishai and all his officials, "My son, who is of my own flesh, is trying to take my life. How much more, then, this Benjamite! Leave him alone; let him curse, for the LORD has told him to.

NIV 2Sa 16:12 It may be that the LORD will see my distress and repay me with good for the cursing I am receiving today."

NIV 2Sa 16:13 So David and his men continued along the road while Shimei was going along the hillside opposite him, cursing as he went and throwing stones at him and showering him with dirt.

NIV 2Sa 16:14 The king and all the people with him arrived at their destination exhausted.

A Psalm Of David

NIV Ps 37:1 Do not fret because of evil men or be envious of those who do wrong;

NIV Ps 37:2 for like the grass they will soon wither, like green plants they will soon die away.

NIV Ps 37:3 Trust in the LORD and do good; dwell in the land and enjoy safe pasture.

NIV Ps 37:4 Delight yourself in the LORD and he will give you the desires of your heart.

NIV Ps 37:5 Commit your way to the LORD; trust in him and he will do this:

NIV Ps 37:6 He will make your righteousness shine like the dawn, the justice of your cause like the noonday sun.

NIV Ps 37:7 Be still before the LORD and wait patiently for him; do not fret when men succeed in their ways, when they carry out their wicked schemes.

NIV Ps 37:8 Refrain from anger and turn from wrath; do not fret—it leads only to evil.

NIV Ps 37:9 For evil men will be cut off, but those who hope in the LORD will inherit the land.

NIV Ps 37:10 A little while, and the wicked will be no more; though you look for them, they will not be found.

NIV Ps 37:11 But the meek will inherit the land and enjoy great peace.

NIV Ps 37:12 The wicked plot against the righteous and gnash their teeth at them;

NIV Ps 37:13 but the Lord laughs at the wicked, for he knows their day is coming.

NIV Ps 37:14 The wicked draw the sword and bend the bow to bring down the poor and needy, to slay those whose ways are upright.

NIV Ps 37:15 But their swords will pierce their own hearts, and their bows will be broken.

NIV Ps 37:16 Better the little that the righteous have than the wealth of many wicked;

NIV Ps 37:17 for the power of the wicked will be broken, but the LORD upholds the righteous.

NIV Ps 37:18 The days of the blameless are known to the LORD, and their inheritance will endure forever.

NIV Ps 37:19 In times of disaster they will not wither; in days of famine they will enjoy plenty.

NIV Ps 37:20 But the wicked will perish: The LORD'S enemies will be like the beauty of the fields, they will vanish—vanish like smoke.

NIV Ps 37:21 The wicked borrow and do not repay, but the righteous give generously; *NIV Ps 37:22* those the LORD blesses will inherit the land, but those he curses will be cut off.

NIV Ps 37:23 If the LORD delights in a man's way, he makes his steps firm; *NIV Ps 37:24* though he stumble, he will not fall, for the LORD upholds him with his hand.

NIV Ps 37:25 I was young and now I am old, yet I have never seen the righteous forsaken or their children begging bread.

NIV Ps 37:26 They are always generous and lend freely; their children will be blessed.

NIV Ps 37:27 Turn from evil and do good; then you will dwell in the land forever.

NIV Ps 37:28 For the LORD loves the just and will not forsake his faithful ones. They will be protected forever, but the offspring of the wicked will be cut off; *NIV Ps 37:29* the righteous will inherit the land and dwell in it forever.

NIV Ps 37:30 The mouth of the righteous man utters wisdom, and his tongue speaks what is just.

NIV Ps 37:31 The law of his God is in his heart; his feet do not slip.

NIV Ps 37:32 The wicked lie in wait for the righteous, seeking their very lives; *NIV Ps 37:33* but the LORD will not leave them in their power or let them be condemned when brought to trial.

NIV Ps 37:34 Wait for the LORD and keep his way. He will exalt you to inherit the land; when the wicked are cut off, you will see it.

NIV Ps 37:35 I have seen a wicked and ruthless man flourishing like a green tree in its native soil,

NIV Ps 37:36 but he soon passed away and was no more; though I looked for him, he could not be found.

NIV Ps 37:37 Consider the blameless, observe the upright; there is a future for the man of peace.

NIV Ps 37:38 But all sinners will be destroyed; the future of the wicked will be cut off.

NIV Ps 37:39 The salvation of the righteous comes from the LORD; he is their stronghold in time of trouble.

NIV Ps 37:40 The LORD helps them and delivers them; he delivers them from the wicked and saves them, because they take refuge in him.

A Psalm of David

NLT Ps 31:1 O LORD, I have come to you for protection; don't let me be put to shame. Rescue me, for you always do what is right.

NLT Ps 31:2 Bend down and listen to me; rescue me quickly. Be for me a great rock of safety, a fortress where my enemies cannot reach me.

NLT Ps 31:3 You are my rock and my fortress. For the honor of your name, lead me out of this peril.

NLT Ps 31:4 Pull me from the trap my enemies set for me, for I find protection in you alone.

NLT Ps 31:5 I entrust my spirit into your hand. Rescue me, LORD, for you are a faithful God.

NLT Ps 31:6 I hate those who worship worthless idols. I trust in the LORD.

NLT Ps 31:7 I am overcome with joy because of your unfailing love, for you have seen my troubles, and you care about the anguish of my soul.

NLT Ps 31:8 You have not handed me over to my enemy but have set me in a safe place.

NLT Ps 31:9 Have mercy on me, LORD, for I am in distress. My sight is blurred because of my tears. My body and soul are withering away.

NLT Ps 31:10 I am dying from grief; my years are shortened by sadness. Misery has drained my strength; I am wasting away from within.

NLT Ps 31:11 I am scorned by all my enemies and despised by my neighbors— even my friends are afraid to come near me. When they see me on the street, they turn the other way.

NLT Ps 31:12 I have been ignored as if I were dead, as if I were a broken pot.

NLT Ps 31:13 I have heard the many rumors about me, and I am surrounded by terror. My enemies conspire against me, plotting to take my life.

NLT Ps 31:14 But I am trusting you, O LORD, saying, "You are my God!"

NLT Ps 31:15 My future is in your hands. Rescue me from those who hunt me down relentlessly.

NLT Ps 31:16 Let your favor shine on your servant. In your unfailing love, save me.

NLT Ps 31:17 Don't let me be disgraced, O LORD, for I call out to you for help. Let the wicked be disgraced; let them lie silent in the grave.

NLT Ps 31:18 May their lying lips be silenced— those proud and arrogant lips that accuse the godly.

NLT Ps 31:19 Your goodness is so great! You have stored up great blessings for those who honor you. You have done so much for those who come to you for protection, blessing them before the watching world.

NLT Ps 31:20 You hide them in the shelter of your presence, safe from those who conspire against them. You shelter them in your presence, far from accusing tongues.

NLT Ps 31:21 Praise the LORD, for he has shown me his unfailing love. He kept me safe when my city was under attack.

NLT Ps 31:22 In sudden fear I had cried out, "I have been cut off from the LORD!" But you heard my cry for mercy and answered my call for help.

NLT Ps 31:23 Love the LORD, all you faithful ones! For the LORD protects those who are loyal to him, but he harshly punishes all who are arrogant.

NLT Ps 31:24 So be strong and take courage, all you who put your hope in the LORD!

Many of the psalms that David wrote have the same theme. This theme in a word, can be described as, "meekness." David may defend the honor of the name of the Lord and protect the Lord's people, but, he does not defend himself, he waits upon the Lord to do so.

Multiple times in his psalms, David asks the Lord to save him for the Lord's namesake. In what way does David think the Lord would be honoring His own name by saving David? He makes it clear in the psalm.

His enemies plot to kill David and they do so out of their own ideas of justice, a justice that serves only themselves. In addition, his enemies plot to kill David and lay traps for him in their own power. David is clear to point this out in his psalms. Conversely, David, in essence, declares that he does not protect himself in his own power. He, in fact, trusts God to protect him. David is not saying to the Lord that because he is such a great person the Lord should save him to protect the honor of His name. No, he is saying his enemies rely on their own strength to kill David. However, he refuses to defend himself in like kind—in his own strength—but instead depends on the Lord to defend him.

As such, if his enemies prevail and kill David, they will be able to brag that they and their idols are stronger than David's God because David relied on his God and was killed anyways. David is saying because I trust in you, God, to defend me and I proclaim and praise your name as the One I trust to protect me, well then, for the sake of bringing honor to your own Name, save me and silence them so I can declare how you defeated my enemies when I relied on You. That is instead of my voice of praise being silenced and them having bragging rights if they were to prevail.

Again, to be poor in spirit and to be meek are tied together. Of the one, Jesus declares the Kingdom of Heaven is theirs. Of the other, He promises they will inherit the earth. In between, He promises that those who mourn will be comforted.

Note: When Matthew talks about the Kingdom in his Gospel he mostly calls it, "the Kingdom of Heaven." On occasion he also calls it, "the Kingdom of God." However, he is the only one of the four writers of the Gospels that calls the Kingdom to come, "the Kingdom of Heaven." The other three Gospels refer to the Kingdom come as, "the Kingdom of God." Both names are referring to the same Kingdom.

When Jesus refers to the Kingdom of Heaven He is talking about a time when He will return to the earth, subdue it, and establish the Kingdom of Heaven here on earth for 1,000 years with Him as King. Jesus calls it the Kingdom of Heaven (the key word being heaven), because it is a celestial or supernatural Kingdom which is housed in the celestial city called, "the New Jerusalem." This city is occupied exclusively with celestial beings:

the Father, Jesus, the angels of the Lord, and celestial humans who have been reclothed with a spiritual body (in order to have a share in the celestial city).

The natural humans alive at that time will continue to live upon the earth under the kingship of the Christ and His celestial humans. The dead who did not qualify to become celestial humans during that time will remain disembodied souls in Hades, unable to participate in the 1,000 year Kingdom of Christ. Then, on the last day of the natural universe, the day of judgment will come. Those in Hades will be resurrected, or reclothed with a body, along with the balance of natural humans that will be alive up to that last day.

Together these two groups will be judged as either (1) fit to be a part of the Kingdom for eternity from that time forward, after the natural universe is destroyed. Or (2), fit to be destroyed in the lake of fire along with the natural universe, fallen angels, and Hades which will be emptied when every soul in it is resurrected to face judgment. Thus suffering a second but permanent death becoming once again a disembodied soul in torment forever as a result of being thrown into the lake of fire.

The Bible, specifically the book of Revelation, is very clear in pointing out that no natural man will or can enter this celestial city or have part in life eternal. The city is made of supernatural matter, unlike our world and our bodies which are made of natural matter. Only celestial beings and celestial humans who possess a body made of supernatural matter can enter into it. Jesus made reference to these conditions when He told the parable of the wedding banquet.

NIV Mt 22:8 "Then he said to his servants, 'The wedding banquet is ready, but those I invited did not deserve to come.*
NIV Mt 22:9 Go to the street corners and invite to the banquet anyone you find.'*

NIV Mt 22:10 *So the servants went out into the streets and gathered all the people they could find, both good and bad, and the wedding hall was filled with guests.*

NIV Mt 22:11 *"But when the king came in to see the guests, he noticed a man there who was not wearing wedding clothes.*

NIV Mt 22:12 *'Friend,' he asked, 'how did you get in here without wedding clothes?' The man was speechless.*

NIV Mt 22:13 *"Then the king told the attendants, 'Tie him hand and foot, and throw him outside, into the darkness, where there will be weeping and gnashing of teeth.'*

NIV Mt 22:14 *"For many are invited, but few are chosen."*

When the Lord describes us as being naked, we are a disembodied soul. We (or our soul—the real man) are clothed with a body. In this parable, when Jesus refers to wedding clothes, He is talking about human souls who are clothed in a celestial body. Many of these guests received their celestial bodies as a part of being raptured. The man who was not clothed with a celestial body was clothed with a natural body. He is thrown out of the New Jerusalem into the world (the natural earth), where the balance of God's wrath is being poured out on the world and on the natural humans who live in it. At this time, the natural earth will be a horrific place to live.

NIV Mt 22:13 *. . . outside, into the darkness, where there will be weeping and gnashing of teeth.'*

A natural human, with a body like ours made of natural matter, could never enter into the New Jerusalem. However, even though His parable reads that a natural man was there inside the city when it is not possible in the first place, Jesus used the image to make that exact point. That image was, a natural human will be restricted from being there. It is just as He spoke to Nicodemus; you must be born of the spirit in order to enter the Kingdom of God. Meaning, you must change your nature from that of being a natural human to that of a celestial human and finally be clothed with a spiritual body, no longer a natural body.

NIV Jn 3:3 *In reply Jesus declared, "I tell you the truth, no one can see the kingdom of God unless he is born again."'*

NIV Jn 3:4 *"How can a man be born when he is old?" Nicodemus asked. "Surely he cannot enter a second time into his mother's womb to be born!"*

NIV Jn 3:5 *Jesus answered, "I tell you the truth, no one can enter the kingdom of God unless he is born of water (even) the Spirit.*

NIV Jn 3:6 *Flesh gives birth to flesh, but the Spirit gives birth to spirit.*

NIV Jn 3:7 *You should not be surprised at my saying, 'You must be born again.'*

Paul calls Jesus the last Adam. He does so because He sees Jesus as the source of a different race, or breed, or nature of humans. When Jesus says, "You must be born again," He is being literal. Meaning, you must be born of a different species of humans, that possess a different nature, a spiritual nature, not a natural nature. To be born again was never meant to be a metaphor of a renewed heart within a man. No, it is actually a literal rebirth of the same personality becoming a different species (for the lack of a better word) of humans.

We were born a natural human through the first Adam, and Jesus recruits individual natural humans to undergo a rebirth and become a celestial human. Same soul, same personality, but new spirit essence, and a new embodiment which is not of this world. It is an embodiment that is not made of natural matter.

This is so important to understand because the entire natural universe is under a death sentence, doomed for destruction. It will become extinct prematurely due to a verdict against it. There is only one way out. That way out is to no longer be a natural human. Without exception, natural humans, along with every molecule of natural matter that make up the universe, will be destroyed.

Jesus is the last Adam because He is the first born celestial human and the source of a new type of human, the celestial human. Celestial humans that are embodied with a body consisting of supernatural matter will transcend the destruction of the natural universe, simply by virtue of the fact that they are not natural—made up of that which is doomed for destruction.

Led by Jesus, the New Jerusalem, along with its inhabitants, will come to the natural earth and rule the earth from that city. The supernatural will cohabitate with the natural for 1,000 years. And during that 1,000 years, His people, the Israelites (natural humans) living during that time, will live in a time of justice, favor and protection from the rest of the world.

If He says the Kingdom of Heaven is ours, it means that we will be one of the celestial humans that live with Jesus in that city, the New Jerusalem, and rule with Him as His ministers over the natural people on the earth. If He says we are to inherit the earth, it is because we will have authority with Jesus over the entire earth and all its natural inhabitants including the Israelites. As celestial humans, we will not even be subject to the weather of the earth or its effects. For it says:

NIV Rev 7:16 Never again will they hunger; never again will they thirst. The sun will not beat upon them, nor any scorching heat.

If He says we are to be comforted, it is because, until that time comes, being poor in spirit and meek will result in the world taking advantage of, dominating, abusing, and enslaving us for their own profit.

If by being poor in spirit and meek we are consequently dominated, we distinguish ourselves as not wanting to enrich our lives as one who fights to posses this present world. Instead, we show ourselves as ones who are living for the world to come. That being the case, we will be in mourning until His Kingdom arrives due to the treatment we receive in this present world because we don't fight for our piece of the pie. In addition, we are aliens in a foreign, desolate, and harsh land which is not our home any longer. The Lord personally wiping away our tears, giving us a part in His celestial Kingdom by giving us a celestial body and authority over the earth, we will indeed be comforted. We will have much more than we could ever amass in the world, and we will have it eternal. For the world is a sinking ship.

NIV Mt 5:6 Blessed are those who hunger and thirst for righteousness, for they will be filled.
NIV Mt 5:7 Blessed are the merciful, for they will be shown mercy.
NIV Mt 5:8 Blessed are the pure in heart, for they will see God.

The pure in heart: When Jesus speaks of the pure in heart, He is not speaking so much of a heart that never does wrong. Although the type of pure heart He is referring to will indeed result in that. What He is really referring to is a heart that purely desires to do the will of God and not his own. He says of those who possess this heart, "they will see God." Scripture also says of life in the New Jerusalem that the celestial humans who reside there will be able to stand before the throne of God and talk with Him face to face. This is what Jesus is referring to when He says, "they will see God."

Jesus said something along the same lines in answer to the religious leaders when they questioned if He and His message were from God.

Amp Jn 7:15 The Jews were astonished. They said, How is it that this Man has learning [is so versed in the sacred Scriptures and in theology] when He has never studied?
Amp Jn 7:16 Jesus answered them by saying, My teaching is not My own, but His Who sent Me.
Amp Jn 7:17 If any man desires to do His will (God's pleasure), he will know (have the needed illumination to recognize, and can tell for himself) whether the teaching

is from God or whether I am speaking from Myself and of My own accord and on My own authority.

Amp Jn 7:18 *He who speaks on his own authority seeks to win honor for himself. [He whose teaching originates with himself seeks his own glory.] But He Who seeks the glory and is eager for the honor of Him Who sent Him, He is true; and there is no unrighteousness or falsehood or deception in Him.*

This is amazing wisdom and insight! Jesus is saying that the person who wants to do the will of the Father—who has a pure heart—will naturally know what is from God and what is not. This is because the things from God will witness to the ones whose will it is to do the will of God. Anything from God will set in his heart as right. The actual words from God will have a satisfying affect to the hungry desire the pure in heart have of wanting to do His will. That satisfying feeling will result in the person having that, "I know that I know" gut feeling that the words are from God.

Conversely, for the ones who have a heart to do their own will, whatever lines up with what they want will witness within their hearts as right and give them a satisfying feeling to the hunger within them that wants to do his own will. Consequently, God's will and words will not have that effect. They will, in fact, be antagonistic towards the one who does not have a pure heart—a desire to do the will of God. This is true for the nonbelievers, the Jews, and the believers who desire to do their own will above that of God's.

This is exactly why Jesus rubbed the Jewish religious leaders the wrong way. It is also why Jesus was able to say of them that, He knew them, and knew that they had no love of God in their hearts! How offensive that must have been to these pious religious leaders of the people of God—but it was true! They did not expose Him as a fraud as they intended, but instead exposed themselves as men who preferred their own will above that of the Lord's, lovers of themselves and of their own lives, not lovers of God, living for Him. All this was true even though they were who they were on the outside.

Jesus is saying that those who have a heart that desires in a holistic or pure way to serve the will of God not only will know His voice and words when they hear them, but will qualify to be chosen as a celestial human in the New Jerusalem, relating to and serving God face to face. They will stand before God and see Him.

NIV Mt 5:9 *Blessed are the peacemakers, for they will be called sons of God.*

To be counted among the sons of God is to be a celestial human. Jesus, the Son of God, was the first born celestial human, and through Him, we are given the right and the way to become a celestial human and thereby be His brothers, the sons of the same Father.

By nature, to be peacemakers in practice is to be poor in spirit and meek. We are to be people of peace if we have the Holy Spirit within. To be a peacemaker is to unify under the authority of the Holy Spirit. To the world, it looks like we are being divisive, arrogant, and unyielding—unwilling to compromise. The reason for this is because, in the world, compromise is the way to peace. You give a little, I give a little, and together we meet in the middle. The righteous who are led by the Spirit will not compromise what they feel the Spirit is instructing. Instead of compromising to gain agreement, they do not advance until all are in agreement as to what the Spirit is saying. This is done through prayer and appealing to God as to what His will is, while laying down personal opinions, objectives, and expertise.

We have a saying in our ministry. "Individual peace feels good, unifying peace stings! But it hurts so good!" That is because to find peace for yourself is to indulge yourself. But to have a unifying peace means to sacrifice your own desires and comfort for the peace and unity of the whole, doing everything not at the pleasure and advantage of serving self, but at the speed of everyone combined together in agreement as one—it stings and causes one to die to self. It causes us to carry not only our own burden, but that of others for the sake of the whole.

NIV Ro 14:17 *For the kingdom of God is not a matter of eating and drinking, but of righteousness (spiritual conformity to God), peace and joy in the Holy Spirit,*
NIV Ro 14:18 *because anyone who serves Christ in this way is pleasing to God and approved by men.*
NIV Ro 14:19 *Let us therefore make every effort to do what leads to peace and to mutual edification.*

Ask any Christian and they will tell you that God hates divorce. However, as an extreme to show the importance of being people of peace, in the case of a spouse who wants to leave the marriage Paul tells us this:

NIV 1Co 7:15 *But if the unbeliever leaves, let him do so. A believing man or woman is not bound in such circumstances; (*Why? Because,*) God has called us to live in peace.*
NIV 1Co 7:16 *How do you know, wife, whether you will save your husband? Or, how do you know, husband, whether you will save your wife?*

Amp Gal 5:25 *If we live by the [Holy] Spirit, let us also walk by the Spirit. [If by the Holy Spirit we have our life in God, let us go forward walking in line, our conduct controlled by the Spirit.]*
Amp Gal 5:26 *Let us not become vainglorious and self-conceited, competitive and challenging and provoking and irritating to one another, envying and being jealous of one another.*
Amp Gal 6:1 *BRETHREN, IF any person is overtaken in misconduct or sin of any sort, you who are spiritual [who are responsive to and controlled by the Spirit] should set him right and restore and reinstate him, without any sense of superiority and with all gentleness, keeping an attentive eye on yourself, lest you should be tempted also.*

Amp Gal 6:2 Bear (endure, carry) one another's burdens and troublesome moral faults, and in this way fulfill and observe perfectly the law of Christ (the Messiah) and complete what is lacking [in your obedience to it].

Amp Gal 6:3 For if any person thinks himself to be somebody [too important to condescend to shoulder another's load] when he is nobody [of superiority except in his own estimation], he deceives and deludes and cheats himself.

Amp Gal 6:4 But let every person carefully scrutinize and examine and test his own conduct and his own work. He can then have the personal satisfaction and joy of doing something commendable [in itself alone] without [resorting to] boastful comparison with his neighbor.

Amp Gal 6:5 For every person will have to bear (be equal to understanding and calmly receive) his own [little] load [of oppressive faults].

Amp Gal 6:6 Let him who receives instruction in the Word [of God] share all good things with his teacher [contributing to his support].

Amp Gal 6:7 Do not be deceived and deluded and misled; God will not allow Himself to be sneered at (scorned, disdained, or mocked by mere pretensions or professions, or by His precepts being set aside.) [He inevitably deludes himself who attempts to delude God.] For whatever a man sows, that and that only is what he will reap.

Amp Gal 6:8 For he who sows to his own flesh (lower nature, sensuality) will from the flesh reap decay and ruin and destruction, but he who sows to the Spirit will from the Spirit reap eternal life.

Amp Gal 6:9 And let us not lose heart and grow weary and faint in acting nobly and doing right, for in due time and at the appointed season we shall reap, if we do not loosen and relax our courage and faint.

Amp Gal 6:10 So then, as occasion and opportunity open up to us, let us do good [morally] to all people [not only being useful or profitable to them, but also doing what is for their spiritual good and advantage]. Be mindful to be a blessing, especially to those of the household of faith [those who belong to God's family with you, the believers].

NIV Mt 5:10 Blessed are those who are persecuted because of righteousness, for theirs is the kingdom of heaven.

NIV Mt 5:11 *"Blessed are you when people insult you, persecute you and falsely say all kinds of evil against you because of me.*
NIV Mt 5:12 *Rejoice and be glad, because great is your reward in heaven, for in the same way they persecuted the prophets who were before you.*

Jesus is saying those who are martyred and persecuted for their faith will receive a spiritual body, thereby becoming a celestial human in the New Jerusalem, and be a part of His Kingdom over the earth for a thousand years, and beyond. That will be their blessing—their reward!

An important thing to take note of here is to realize about verses 10, 11, and 12 that it is more than a profession of faith that one would be persecuted for and for which people would lie about you. In the next verses, concerning the salt and the light, the spiritual man is discussed. In describing the spiritual man, it is discussed how he is thoroughly misunderstood and his motives a mystery. We are told in Scripture that no one can get insight into the spiritual man. Consequently, the spiritual man is not trusted, held suspect, constantly misunderstood, and accused falsely for the motives behind what he says or does.

One of the biggest issues the spiritual man has with people of the world is that they are forever accusing him of having motives and reasons for his decisions that are not true. This is because the spiritual man does the Lord's will and not his own. However, people of the world cannot fathom that he would make a decision based on the will of God and not based on his own desires or wants. This issue is discussed below; however, how it pertains to persecution is, first off, that worldly people take the spiritual man's decisions as a reflection on themselves. They take his decision personal and think it is based on how he feels personally about them.

Therefore, there is a huge temptation to give a reasonable answer they can accept (in their minds) as to why the spiritual man would make that decision, as well as, to compromise what the Holy Spirit is saying so as not to offend. "Is it because you are mad at me? Or because you like them better than me?" The temptation comes in, and when he is faced to answer, there is a pressure for him to give a worldly reason. For example, "it is too far to travel," or "I have to work that day." It's easy to do because they won't understand or accept, "because the Lord told me not to come." But the true spiritual man, at the risk of offending, tells the truth about the reasons behind his decisions.

As a result, there is a pressure accompanied by false accusations and persecution to do what will make the worldly person happy. The spiritual man will be labeled as unwilling to compromise, stubborn, uncaring, arrogant and disloyal. It may not be life and death as some believers face; nevertheless, it is a very real challenge to stand firm in obedience to the Holy Spirit.

Salt and Light

NIV Mt 5:13 *"You are the salt of the earth. But if the salt loses its saltiness, how can it be made salty again? It is no longer good for anything, except to be thrown out and trampled by men."*

Jesus quite often cloaks profound truths and prophecies in metaphors and parables. Verse 13 is a good example. What He says about salt which loses its saltiness is a reference to judgment that is to come against the worldly Church. Jesus is saying that His Church is the salt of the earth. Most certainly He is talking about the Church's preserving or saving effect on the rest of the people in the world. This is verified by the very next verses (14 and 15) where He refers to the Church again as light for the world.

When salt loses its preserving effect on food to keep it from spoiling and, therefore, becomes inedible, well then, salt may still be salt but it is rendered useless and is no longer good for the purpose it was employed or made for. Jesus is telling us that we, His Church, are on the earth for a reason. That reason is to preserve (or save) the people of the earth. When we lose our ability to do so, we might be the Church, but we are rendered useless for the reason we were destined. He is predicting a time in the future from when He spoke these words. He goes on to say " . . . It (salt) is no longer good for anything, except to be thrown out and trampled by men." It has to be asked; why say, " except to be thrown out and trampled by men?" Why not say that it is no longer good for anything, or it is good only to be disposed of? Why add, "to be trampled by men?" These are condemning words.

The Jews turned on Jesus and would not answer His call, so He turned to the gentiles. And now Jesus is saying the Church will become useless as well. If, as a Church, we do not fulfill our purpose, we are useless to the plan of salvation for the world, and we are no longer what we were to be to Christ, thus rendered useless to Him. However, it doesn't stop at the Church being discarded by Jesus. He goes on to say we will be "trampled by men." What does this mean? The book of Revelation helps us understand when He uses the same wording.

Amp Rev 11:1 *A REED [as a measuring rod] was then given to me, [shaped] like a staff, and I was told: Rise up and measure the sanctuary of God and the altar [of incense], and [number] those who worship there.*
Amp Rev 11:2 *But leave out of your measuring the court outside the sanctuary of God; omit that, for it is given over to the Gentiles (the nations), and they will trample the holy city underfoot for 42 months (three and one-half years).*

These verses are talking about a time to come when John is given a standard by which to measure or judge those who worship God in intimate union with Him, and number them—to identify them. This is a reference to what is known as the rapture. These numbers or people will be lifted up receiving a celestial body and never experience death or what is to come. However, those who are called believers and do not have an intimate relationship of union with Him are represented as being the outer court of the sanctuary. They are the numbers who comprise the worldly Church and will be discarded as salt losing its saltiness. They will be given over to the non-believers in order to be trampled on (killed) for 3-1/2 years. This is the time period of the great tribulation. Notice how the word "trample on" is used in reference to the tribulation time period of 3-1//2 years. Again, Revelation goes over this prophetic judgment to come:

The Harvest of the Earth

NIV Rev 14:12 *This calls for patient endurance on the part of the saints who obey God's commandments and remain faithful to Jesus.*

NIV Rev 14:13 *Then I heard a voice from heaven say, "Write: Blessed are the dead who die in the Lord from now on." "Yes," says the Spirit, "they will rest from their labor, for their deeds will follow them."*

NIV Rev 14:14 *I looked, and there before me was a white cloud, and seated on the cloud was one "like a son of man" with a crown of gold on his head and a sharp sickle in his hand.*

NIV Rev 14:15 *Then another angel came out of the temple and called in a loud voice to him who was sitting on the cloud, "Take your sickle and reap, because the time to reap has come, for the harvest of the earth is ripe."*

NIV Rev 14:16 *So he who was seated on the cloud swung his sickle over the earth, and the earth was harvested.*

NIV Rev 14:17 *Another angel came out of the temple in heaven, and he too had a sharp sickle.*

NIV Rev 14:18 *Still another angel, who had charge of the fire, came from the altar and called in a loud voice to him who had the sharp sickle, "Take your sharp sickle and gather the clusters of grapes from the earth's vine, because its grapes are ripe."*

NIV Rev 14:19 *The angel swung his sickle on the earth, gathered its grapes and threw them into the great winepress of God's wrath.*

NIV Rev 14:20 *They were trampled in the winepress outside the city, and blood flowed out of the press, rising as high as the horses' bridles for a distance of 1,600 stadia* (about 200 miles).

The above verses concerning the harvest of the earth describe two different means of harvest, just as the previous verses did. Those who are harvested as wheat (inferred, not said) will become celestial humans and a part of Jesus' 1,000 year Kingdom from Heaven. The first type of harvest is performed by Jesus.

Rev 14:14 *I looked, and there before me was a white cloud, and seated on the cloud was one "like a son of man" with a crown of gold on his head and a sharp sickle in his hand.*

This type of harvest that Jesus performs is in actuality, the rapture. The second type of harvest is performed by men, given a power and directed by an angel. It is the beast who kills the believers during the 3-1/2 year tribulation.

NIV Rev 14:18 *Still another angel, who had charge of the fire, came from the altar and called in a loud voice to him who had the sharp sickle, "Take your sharp sickle and gather the clusters of grapes from the earth's vine, because its grapes are ripe."*
NIV Rev 14:19 *The angel swung his sickle on the earth, gathered its grapes and threw them into the great winepress of God's wrath.*
NIV Rev 14:20 *They were trampled in the winepress outside the city, and blood flowed out of the press, rising as high as the horses' bridles for a distance of 1,600 stadia* (about 200 miles).

It's significant that Jesus refers to the second harvest as grapes. This is because the way that grapes were made to give up their juice is for them to be trampled underfoot until all of the juice is squeezed out of them. Jesus outright says that juice is the blood of those who are harvested by these means. In other words, He is continuing the metaphor that He started with salt. And that is to say, the salt of the earth that loses its saltiness is only good to be discarded and trampled on. These two metaphors help us understand that the grapes which are trampled on are the *Church Corrupt* and not people in the world.

These grapes who are trampled on and whose combined blood flows like a river about four to five feet deep for 200 miles are the believers left behind to suffer the tribulation. The bad news is that they will be tormented and lose their lives when the world turns against them. The good news is that they, too, will be harvested and qualify to become a celestial human who will rule the earth together for 1,000 years. For it says about them:

NIV Rev 14:12 This calls for patient endurance on the part of the saints who obey God's commandments and remain faithful to Jesus.
NIV Rev 14:13 Then I heard a voice from heaven say, "Write: Blessed are the dead who die in the Lord from now on." "Yes," says the Spirit, "they will rest from their labor, for their deeds will follow them."

And again:

The Great Multitude in White Robes

NIV Rev 7:9 After this I looked and there before me was a great multitude that no one could count, from every nation, tribe, people and language, standing before the throne and in front of the Lamb. They were wearing white robes (Meaning now clothed in a celestial body) *and were holding palm branches in their hands.*

Note: Verse 9 says the number of the great multitude cannot be counted because there were so many. What we do know is that there was enough blood spilled to create a river that flowed 200 miles and 4-5 feet deep on average. For reference sake, there is about ten pints of blood in each human, that is a gallon and a quart. How many deaths must it take to create a river of blood 200 miles long and 4-5 feet deep? That is a lot of killing within a 3 1/2 year time period. It would seem that the majority of the Christian Church will gain their celestial bodies through being purified with fire by enduring the great tribulation. It stands to reason that it is a smaller contingency of Christians who will avoid the great tribulation by being harvested as wheat and brought up to be stored in His barn (in Heaven) during that time through the rapture.

NIV Rev 7:10 And they cried out in a loud voice: "Salvation belongs to our God, who sits on the throne, and to the Lamb."

NIV Rev 7:11 All the angels were standing around the throne and around the elders and the four living creatures. They fell down on their faces before the throne and worshiped God,

NIV Rev 7:12 saying: "Amen! Praise and glory and wisdom and thanks and honor and power and strength be to our God for ever and ever. Amen!"

NIV Rev 7:13 Then one of the elders asked me, "These in white robes—who are they, and where did they come from?"

NIV Rev 7:14 I answered, "Sir, you know." And he said, "These are they who have come out of the great tribulation; they have washed their robes and made them white in the blood of the Lamb.

NIV Rev 7:15 Therefore, "they are before the throne of God and serve him day and night in his temple; and he who sits on the throne will spread his tent over them.

NIV Rev 7:16 Never again will they hunger; never again will they thirst. The sun will not beat upon them, nor any scorching heat.

NIV Rev 7:17 For the Lamb at the center of the throne will be their shepherd; he will lead them to springs of living water. And God will wipe away every tear from their eyes."

NIV Mt 5:14 "You are the light of the world. A city on a hill cannot be hidden.

NIV Mt 5:15 Neither do people light a lamp and put it under a bowl. Instead they put it on its stand, and it gives light to everyone in the house.

NIV Mt 5:16 *In the same way, let your light shine before men, that they may see your good deeds and praise your Father in heaven.*

John's Gospel has a verse which gives us insight into what Jesus says about light:

Amp Jn 3:19 *The [basis of the] judgment (indictment, the test by which men are judged, the ground for the sentence) lies in this: the Light has come into the world, and people have loved the darkness rather than and more than the Light, for their works (deeds) were evil.*
Amp Jn 3:20 *For every wrongdoer hates (loathes, detests) the Light, and will not come out into the Light but shrinks from it, lest his works (his deeds, his activities, his conduct) be exposed and reproved.*
Amp Jn 3:21 *But he who practices truth [who does what is right] comes out into the Light; so that his works may be plainly shown to be what they are—wrought with God [divinely prompted, done with God's help, in dependence upon Him].*

The light that came into the world is the Spirit of Jesus. It is the same Spirit which shines from within us as we who are in union with Him give expression to Him through our lives in the body. That light is an enlightened consciousness which illuminates, exposes, and convicts the thoughts and purposes of the heart. It shows the spirit of this world within the human spirit as in defiance to God and false to the truth. It shows people of the world as lovers of themselves, selfish, and self-centered, perceiving everything in light of how it makes them feel, and in light of how everything effects them. Their sense of right and wrong is exclusively based on that, which is a lie by nature.

The man who lives in the light, worshiping the Lord in Spirit and in truth, Paul calls, a "spiritual man." The spiritual man is that city on a hill, that lamp which the Lord puts on a lamp stand. Through no fault or agenda of his own, even while going about his own business of trying to hear, interpret, and respond to the Holy Spirit, his Holy Spirit responses bring to light the true heart motives and purposes of all he comes in contact with. Of him, Paul says he has the Holy Spirit of God, and thus, can know the thoughts of God. He also has the mind of Christ and holds the thoughts, feelings, and purposes of His heart. Meaning, he has a sense of the heart of Jesus, and then after identifying with it, he responds out of the thoughts, feelings and purposes of Jesus, not his own.

Amp 1Co 2:15 *But the spiritual man tries all things [he examines, investigates, inquires into, questions, and discerns all things], yet is himself to be put on trial and judged by no one [he can read the meaning of everything, but no one can properly discern or appraise or get an insight into him].*
Amp 1Co 2:16 *For who has known or understood the mind (the counsels and purposes) of the Lord so as to guide and instruct Him and give Him knowledge? But we have the mind of Christ (the Messiah) and do hold the thoughts (feelings and purposes) of His heart.*

The spiritual man—the bearer of light—is generous, unselfish, kind, honest, most often direct, ever ready to sacrifice for others, and willing to carry the burdens of others. However, because of a subtle difference about him, distinguishing him from the men of the world, he is generally not trusted and most often held suspect. This holds true even when it comes to the worldly Church—they don't trust him either.

In fact, adulterers, liars, thieves, and those who exploit others for personal gain are trusted more than spiritual men and women. There is a reason for this phenomena. Paul spoke the reason above: . . . *[he* (the spiritual man) *can read the meaning of everything, but no one can properly discern or appraise or get an insight into him].* Below are listed a few effects of people not getting insight into the spiritual man.

1) People, in general, do not trust anyone they can't get any insight into. It is also difficult for most people to fathom that people can have thoughts or wisdom or reason outside of what they personally have. If they can't

get a read on a person, it leaves them unsettled, even afraid of them, and unable to trust them. A typical result is to assign motives, like throwing mud against the wall to see what sticks.

2) People assume the spiritual man is hiding something, and that's why they can't get a read on him.

3) They believe that what the spiritual man does for others somehow has to be done with ulterior motives; in the end, he is serving his own interest.

4) Because of the worldly spirit all people perceive and operate out of, it is beyond their comprehension that a person can live to satisfy the will of something other than themselves. It never occurs to them that someone can live that way; they always assume everyone does everything ultimately for their own benefit. However, if it were possible for them to imagine someone living for the will of another, they would see that way as being brainwashed or under some kind of mind control. They are forever ascribing incorrect reason for why the spiritual man does what he does, in addition to always taking their decisions personal.

For example, a spiritual man prays and senses that the Holy Spirit does not want him to go out to a certain event that a certain friend has invited him to. So the spiritual man turns him down. The friend takes it personal and wonders why he doesn't want to go out with him. "Are you mad at me? Don't you like me anymore? I thought we were friends?" The spiritual man may have no reason why it makes sense, other than that he felt a check from the Holy Spirit not to go. To a worldly friend who wants you to go, that is not satisfactory. In their mind, there has to be a reason you will not go. This is because they can't conceive of any rational reason why something would hold them back, and they most often assume it has to do with how you feel towards him. In fact, when the spiritual man doesn't come up with a reasonable explanation, the friend assumes it is because he doesn't want to tell him the real reason. He then takes the quantum leap of thinking the spiritual man doesn't want to tell him the real reason because he doesn't think well of him.

There was this one case where the worldly person kept pressuring the spiritual man for a reason. "Don't you like hanging with me anymore?" "No, that's not it," he answered. "Are you mad at me?" "I prayed about it, and I felt like the Holy Spirit was saying for me to not go." "That's not a reason, why would the Holy Spirit tell you not to come? Did He tell you not to come because you are mad at me?" (This was an actual conversation between a spiritual man and a worldly man).

People of the world will not only take the decisions of the spiritual man personally, but find it almost impossible to comprehend that the spiritual man's decision is based on something other than personal reasons. The truth is, however, he does what he does because he is single-minded. He is determined to search out the Lord's will and make sure he doesn't fail at satisfying that. He will do things he doesn't want to do from a personal standpoint, and he will not do the things he personally wants to do if it is not the Spirit's will. He really does not concern himself with what he wants, but with what the Holy Spirit wants. As subtle of a heart posture difference this is from the people of the world, it has huge implications when it comes to living in harmony and agreement with worldly-minded people.

According to the way of the spiritual man, it matters little how things turn out: seemingly good or seemingly bad, profitable for him personally, or his life and resources poured out for seemingly nothing—like a drink offering. His reward is not any accomplishment, praise, profit, or position, but that He pleases the Lord by embodying His Spirit, giving expression to God's will through his own life in the body. The two become closer (even as one whole person), as a result.

5) People don't know what they don't know. It also says that to the corrupt, all things are corrupt. People can witness or know about an act done in purity with unselfish reasons by the spiritual man, but they can only understand that act to be done for corrupt and self-gratifying reasons. It can actually be impossible for them to see certain acts in any other light because of their own defects. As such, and when they can't figure out the spiritual man, they ascribe reason and motives to the spiritual man that they themselves would have if they did the same things.

In group settings, and in community, the spiritual man holds only the agenda of God and not that of the group if it does not align with the Spirit. We have already covered how the universal way of unity to the world includes compromise. However, the spiritual man never compromises, but only does as he feels the Spirit is directing him. In the case of disagreement, he seeks out the Lord's will in objective prayer along with the other members involved until they all agree on a course of action that they unanimously believe is the direction of the Spirit. But since he does not compromise, the worldly mind sees him as an unyielding, inconsiderate, selfish, arrogant know-it-all.

Peter says of the spiritual man:

Amp 1Pe 4:4 *They are astonished and think it very queer that you do not now run hand in hand with them in the same excesses of dissipation, and they abuse [you].*

Amp 1Pe 4:5 *But they will have to give an account to Him Who is ready to judge and pass sentence on the living and the dead.*

Amp 1Pe 4:6 *For this is why the good news (the Gospel) was preached [in their lifetime] even to the dead, that though judged in fleshly bodies as men are, they might live in the spirit as God does.*

The spiritual man becomes detached from the things of this world. He is easily moved by the Spirit, because he has less and less of the cares of this world anchoring him down as he grows in his faith. He is ready to be content in all things and in every situation.

The spiritual man is only really understood by God Himself, who is in spiritual union with him. He is also understood by others who are spiritual, but not by worldly Christians any more than by non-Christians. Paul says of non-spiritual men in the church:

NIV 1Co 3:1 *Brothers, I could not address you as spiritual but as worldly—mere infants in Christ.*
NIV 1Co 3:2 *I gave you milk, not solid food, for you were not yet ready for it. Indeed, you are still not ready.*
NIV 1Co 3:3 *You are still worldly. For since there is jealousy and quarreling among you, are you not worldly? Are you not acting like mere men?*
NIV 1Co 3:4 *For when one says, "I follow Paul," and another, "I follow Apollos," u are you not mere men?*

Judging by these words, Paul considers that a true Christian, a spiritual man, has evolved into something way beyond a human person of the world. Indeed they have! After they have finally received their resurrected body, the process becomes complete and they are fully evolved into celestial humans, who are in union with God. Jesus tells us we actually become children of God, and we should not call anyone on earth father anymore, because God is our Father.

Amp Jn 3:6 *What is born of [from] the flesh is flesh [of the physical is physical]; and what is born of the Spirit is spirit.*
Amp Jn 3:7 *Marvel not [do not be surprised, astonished] at My telling you, You must all be born anew (from above).*

Amp Jn 3:8 *The wind blows (breathes) where it wills; and though you hear its sound, yet you neither know where it comes from nor where it is going. So it is with everyone who is born of the Spirit.*

Amp Jn 3:9 *Nicodemus answered by asking, How can all this be possible?*

Amp Jn 3:10 *Jesus replied, Are you the teacher of Israel, and yet do not know nor understand these things? [Are they strange to you?]*

Amp Jn 3:11 *I assure you, most solemnly I tell you, We speak only of what we know [we know absolutely what we are talking about]; we have actually seen what we are testifying to [we were eyewitnesses of it]. And still you do not receive our testimony [you reject and refuse our evidence—that of Myself and of all those who are born of the Spirit].*

Amp Jn 3:12 *If I have told you of things that happen right here on the earth and yet none of you believes Me, how can you believe (trust Me, adhere to Me, rely on Me) if I tell you of heavenly things?*

The Fulfillment of the Law

NIV Mt 5:17 *"Do not think that I have come to abolish the Law or the Prophets; I have not come to abolish them but to fulfill them.*

NIV Mt 5:18 *I tell you the truth, until heaven and earth disappear, not the smallest letter, not the least stroke of a pen, will by any means disappear from the Law until everything is accomplished.*

NIV Mt 5:19 *Anyone who breaks one of the least of these commandments and teaches others to do the same will be called least in the kingdom of heaven, but whoever practices and teaches these commands will be called great in the kingdom of heaven.*

NIV Mt 5:20 *For I tell you that unless your righteousness surpasses that of the Pharisees and the teachers of the law, you will certainly not enter the kingdom of heaven.*

In verses 17-20, Jesus tells us that He is not trying to change or negate the law of Moses. We have already explained how and why this is true. However, as an additional note, it is significant to recognize that Jesus speaks these words right before He talks about seemingly raising the bar of the law when it comes to murder, adultery, divorce etc.. He is making it clear that He is teaching us the spiritual, or righteous requirements of the law so we may be enlightened and understand how to function as spiritual men. For soon we will actually have celestial bodies living in the spiritual realm, and we will need to keep within the boundaries of the spiritual realm—the realm which Jesus and His Father rule from.

He said:

NIV Jn 14:23 *Jesus replied, "If anyone loves me, he will obey my teaching. My Father will love him, and we will come to him and make our home with him.*
NIV Jn 14:24 *He who does not love me will not obey my teaching. These words you hear are not my own; they belong to the Father who sent me.*

Jesus doesn't say, "obey My law," but "obey My teaching." This is in keeping with what He says in verses 17-20. He is not reinventing the law, but teaching us the spiritual aspect of it. He is acting as an advanced teacher of the law and not a law maker. In verses 23 and 24, He is promising that if we live life as an enlightened spiritual man, observant of the spiritual aspect of the law which He taught us, then He and His Father, through their Spirit, will come to us, live in us, and be in union with us. This guarantees that we will be celestial beings when all is said and done.

Murder

NIV Mt 5:21 *"You have heard that it was said to the people long ago, 'Do not murder, and anyone who murders will be subject to judgment.'*
NIV Mt 5:22 *But I tell you that anyone who is angry with his brother will be subject to judgment. Again, anyone who says to his brother, 'Raca,' is answerable to the Sanhedrin. But anyone who says, 'You fool!' will be in danger of the fire of hell.*
NIV Mt 5:23 *"Therefore, if you are offering your gift at the altar and there remember that your brother has something against you,*

NIV Mt 5:24 leave your gift there in front of the altar. First go and be reconciled to your brother; then come and offer your gift.

NIV Mt 5:25 "Settle matters quickly with your adversary who is taking you to court. Do it while you are still with him on the way, or he may hand you over to the judge, and the judge may hand you over to the officer, and you may be thrown into prison.

NIV Mt 5:26 I tell you the truth, you will not get out until you have paid the last penny.

It was already covered how Jesus is not simply upping the standards, but educating us on the "righteous requirements," or the spiritual aspect, of the law. When we think of murder, we think of ending a person's life by killing the body. Although that is the case, it is a superficial view of murder. Jesus was trying to help us understand that when we hate or despise a person in our heart, we cut that person off. Although that person may live, he becomes dead to us. In this way, we are guilty of murder, according to the laws of God.

We hate to see that person have any success in their life, be nurtured, or even for others to care about him or support him. To know of any of this happening to him, we become jealous and angry. We might not be plunging a knife into his chest, but in our own heart we render him as dead. Even if we don't outwardly declare him dead, we would rather have the life strangled out of him than see him prosper.

It is not just a standard of niceness God is holding us to, but a heart posture. Spiritually speaking, Jesus is making us aware that we are murderers in our own spirit when we hate or revel in denying nurturing for someone and desire or make someone dead to ourselves even while they live on.

In addition, to injure a person by demeaning him and projecting onto him that he has no value can kill the person's esteem of himself. He might still be living and breathing, but become traumatized in his spirit, losing self-worth and, in turn, losing hope, living life without ambition or inspiration. Jesus is saying be careful; you might think you are frustrated with a person and just blowing off a little steam and don't mean anything by it (it's not like you hit him or something), however, you may carelessly crush his spirit and destroy, even kill, his personality. We can't know, what we say could be the last straw which destroys a person's self-esteem. For this outcome, being upset with him is not an excuse. By virtue of how his Creator embraces him, a human personality is worthy of much more respect, tolerance, and care than many of us would like to behold him with.

Again, it is the invisible nature of a man (or the spiritual aspect of him) that Jesus is trying to help us see is as real and as important to respect as the body of the person. And we cannot let ourselves think that how we treat the invisible nature of the man—his mind and spirit—is any less critical than how we treat his body. They both can be injured, crippled, even killed. Furthermore, to be spiritual in our perception is to understand that it is not how we judge or what we think of a person which counts and defines his value, but instead, it is how his Creator beholds the person He created.

The second part of this teaching should be quite obvious. It's like a person comes to honor you and give you a gift to show his love and respect for you. However, that person has been abusive both in speaking to and in treatment of your wife. That person should not believe his gift and honor will curry any favor for him with you. In fact, you would receive his honor and gift with contempt, as an insult. That person would do well to settle his issue with your wife even before you found out about it and especially before he would encounter you. In doing so, when he would finally face you, your anger over his treatment of your wife would be tempered by the fact that they worked out everything, and it is now all water under the bridge.

Jesus is basically saying the same thing to those who would honor God but treat His children with contempt. Spiritually speaking, we have to account for our treatment of our fellow humans to God their Father. It is written that whoever takes the life of a human being will have to answer to God directly for this offense. There are situations where taking a life would be justified. However, it is not a trivial matter, because the Lord holds precious the life of a human, for we were made in His image.

Adultery

NIV Mt 5:27 "You have heard that it was said, 'Do not commit adultery.'

NIV Mt 5:28 But I tell you that anyone who looks at a woman lustfully has already committed adultery with her in his heart.

NIV Mt 5:29 If your right eye causes you to sin, gouge it out and throw it away. It is better for you to lose one part of your body than for your whole body to be thrown into hell.

NIV Mt 5:30 And if your right hand causes you to sin, cut it off and throw it away. It is better for you to lose one part of your body than for your whole body to go into hell.

Again, Jesus is showing us spiritual conformity to a law which is in place and not simply making stricter standards to live by. In doing so, He is teaching us a new perception of life which is spiritual and not superficial or unspiritual. He is also making us aware of what the spiritual realities look like for those who would want to be enlightened spiritually.

Unspiritual or worldly people associate spirit energy and power as feelings. Psychology, for example, is a practice that doesn't acknowledge spirit or the spirit of a man and, as a result, understands the man's spirit as the subconscious or unconscious mind. In addition, it understands the mind to be the brain or a function of the brain. However, the mind is the soul. It is not the brain but a separate nature than the body with its brain. Feelings are really a discerning sense of the quality of spirit energy. Feelings are a sense of spirit energy like sight is a sense of the different hues of color within light.

Being unspiritual, the affects our spiritual energy have on each other is grossly underestimated, even not recognized. Again, worldly people may think that their spirit energies are simply their own feelings and that they are private. However, when they feel lust towards another person and fantasize about them, they are, first of all, stirring up their spirit energy to overwhelming levels. Secondly, they are projecting on to them their spirit energy and consciousness (awareness). Invisible and disembodied as their spirit consciousness is, the conscious energy is as real as and has an impact every bit as powerful as invisible electricity.

Scripture says there is no time or distance in the spirit. That is because spirit is not an object like a body. It doesn't have to transport from one place to another to be there. We always propose the question, "How can you be with someone in spirit?" The answer, we tell them, is to think about them—to direct feelings and thoughts towards them. As Paul spoke:

NIV 1Co 5:3 *Even though I am not physically present, I am with you in spirit.*

It is common that people often come to mind right before you get a phone call from them. This is because when the person calling you decides to pick up his phone to dial, he has decided to direct his thoughts and feelings (spirit energy) towards you. Since there is no time or distance in the spirit, as soon as he starts reaching out by directing his focus towards you, he is actually there with you before the phone rings, even before he starts to dial. He is present with you from the time he has committed in his mind to pick up the phone and dial.

When you are alone in your bedroom, and you fantasize about someone, letting yourself have imaginings, even going as far as gratifying yourself over them, you may think it was a private moment that you had and it didn't involve or harm anyone else. However, that truly is not the case, spiritually speaking.

First of all, you may have had restraint by not touching the person in an inappropriate way, objectifying them and taking advantage of them. However, you have shown no such restraint in your spirit with your spirit energies (feelings).

Likewise, you may think that you were alone and harmed no one, but your feelings of lust, objectification, inappropriate boundaries, and imaginings are, first of all, intense and powerful spirit energies. The ensuing feelings are simply your sense of the qualities of those energies. More importantly, those energies do assault the person lusted after. Those who understand everything in a non-spiritual way will experience your lustful energies as their own and either struggle with them because of their own principles and moralities, or be moved by them and be overcome by lust themselves.

Lastly, you may think that what you let yourself feel and imagine doesn't count because you never touched the person and it was just in your mind (no harm, no foul), but spirit energies are real, every bit as much as what transpires outwardly. This is why Jesus says that if you let your mind and heart go there and cross those boundaries, spiritually speaking, you have assaulted them and broken the spiritual aspect of the same law which governs your behavior. Simply put, you let your spirit cross boundaries you would not allow your body to cross because you understand them to be wrong.

If you have spiritual sight, these things become very real; they become something beyond a personal experience done in private in just the mind of the person. Let's say, for example, a person has an issue with viewing pornography. It becomes distracting for us, because when we look at them, we will see male or female genitalia in front of the person's face, depending on what they obsess over. It is like an image that was left on a computer monitor for too long and that image burned itself on the monitor. You can still see other things, but that image is right there overlaying everything. It's strange to be talking to someone about something serious, or about God, or about morality, and see a sex organ in front of the person's face that won't go away because that is mostly what they think about, imagine, view, and fantasize about.

It is a different story altogether when someone lets themselves lust and fantasize over you. You can see, experience, and have a sense of their lust in a couple different ways, depending how you primarily sense spirit energies and according to your own personal moralities. To us, it feels and looks like a fifthly, lustful, blob-like slime. It's a cloud-like energy which is directed towards sex organs that won't go away until the person stops lusting or their thoughts are distracted and directed somewhere else. We also see a picture, or a clip, or have a knowing of who the source person is, projecting his lust in our direction.

This makes it awkward when relating to the person when you see him later. It feels like there is an elephant in the room that nobody is talking about. It's hard to think of and treat this person as normal when we encounter them. We know what we pick up is accurate, so we are not afraid to confront the person and make them aware we feel violated. When we do so, most often, and because of the way we approach them, they admit to it and repent.

After all this, the non-spiritual person will say, "I can't help it; it's what I feel. What am I supposed to do?" This is a pitiful response. It's like a fellow who says, "I can't help it, it hurts when the car tires roll over my toes." Well, you may be right that you can't help that it hurts, but you could move your foot so the tires don't roll over your toes.

When someone says they can't help how they feel as if it means they have no choice but to gratify those feelings, we ask them what happens when they feel like they have to go to the bathroom and have an urge to do so. Do you say you can't help it and just make a mess wherever you are? No, in your lifetime you have learned restraint, even continence, giving expression to those bathroom urges and feelings only where and when it is appropriate. They say, "yeah but the feeling doesn't go away." To which we answer, "Neither do the urges or feelings of having to go to the bathroom when you restrain yourself from making a mess."

The point is, if your mind can have a control and restrain the feelings and urges of the body, then it can of the spirit feelings and energies. Jesus is saying the same thing by teaching us that we are still sinning and assaulting someone if we let ourselves lust after them, even if we didn't do so through our outward behavior. And that it is just as serious of an affront as doing so to the body. In other words, the spiritual is real, and it does count.

Divorce

NIV Mt 5:31 *"It has been said, 'Anyone who divorces his wife must give her a certificate of divorce.*
NIV Mt 5:32 *But I tell you that anyone who divorces his wife, except for marital unfaithfulness, causes her to become an adulteress, and anyone who marries the divorced woman commits adultery.*

Once we take wedding vows, the Lord agrees with us, and reconciles the two lives as one. They both stop living as individuals, each pursuing a life of their own. Through their marriage, the two individuals live instead for a common life. What they work for is no longer self, but for this common life they share. She may manage the home and the children. He may work and earn money to live on. However, whatever they do works for this common life they have together, not for their own enrichment. When they stood before God and made their vows to each other, He agreed from that time on that the two share one common life—the two are one.

It was God who created us as individuals, and when we make a vow before God with a marriage partner, it is He who reconciles us as one from that time forth. Our status, even our identity with our own Creator, changes. And how God sees things is the reality of our existence. This is a Spiritual reality even more than it is a physical reality.

Here is what is important to understand: Just because we desire to move on doesn't necessarily change God's decision when He declared the two one. According to Jesus in these verses, just because we got a divorce in court doesn't mean God, too, has changed the way He bounded the two as one. In the natural or visible world, we may have decided we no longer want to be married to that individual for whatever reasons, get a divorce, move on, and perhaps marry someone else more to our liking. However, we completely ignore the spiritual (who we made a vow before and who changed the status of our identity). To be divorced, the spiritual needs to be reconciled even as it is needed in civil court. Given what Jesus says is the case if someone marries your ex-wife, from a spiritual standpoint, she and her new husband become adulterers, and you share the guilt.

How can this be the case when you have nothing to do with her anymore? It is the case; just because you changed your mind and a court agrees and honors your separation doesn't mean God is obligated to follow your decisions. His integrity, faithfulness, and honor runs deeper than ours. He continues to see the two as one until He has just cause why He should see the two any different. Us moving on doesn't change Him and His ethics (for a lack of a better word). It is frivolous and shallow-minded (unspiritual) for us to only consider our actions in light of how they serve us. This is exactly the case for worldly-minded people who operate under the defect.

As Jesus points out, if we change our marital status without consulting and getting agreement from God and He does not see the status of the two any different, just because you move on and start a new life, doesn't mean God sees your new life as your true status. As such, you would make your wife an adulteress, as well as the man who would marry her, thinking she was single (as we already outlined). However, as a result, you share in their sin. In addition, your new life is completely outside the bounds of the will and structure God holds for your life. You are in complete rebellion. Yet all you see is your situation, improved from what it was, and you are pleased. Spiritually speaking, your life has completely disconnected from God, and He is no longer part of what you are living out. He understands your life in a completely different way than you do. You are living a life completely free from Him even if you attend church and are religious.

One might say, "I don't believe in God." However, that won't make Him disappear or negate His reality for your life. In addition to that "out of touch with spiritual reality" outlook, you made a vow to God in marrying your wife while standing before Him, a legal representative of a worldly court, and many invited witnesses. Now that you have changed your mind, do you only have to change that status with a worldly court? Jesus, in essence, is telling us, "No, that is not the case!"

Divorce is an amazing example of how the defect has blinded us to the spiritual. We have rendered the spiritual insignificant in our hearts. Jesus using divorce as a real life example, to teach us the spiritual implications of what we do on earth, is a wonderful way to help us begin to view life as a spiritual man. In other words, we need to become aware of the spiritual and know that our own estimations, judgments, and decisions are not the only ones involved. In addition, we can learn from this example that it is the Lord's judgments and decisions that count.

It has been our experience that once a person gives his life over to God he may conceivably face many years of loss and upheaval until his life lines up with the reality God views and wills for it to be. This is all part of reconciling with the one true God and his spiritual reality for our lives.

We, as humans, are so out of sync with God's reality for our lives. We see our lives as a pursuit for happiness. God knows that this world is doomed for destruction and all in it. We cry and struggle against seemingly unjust and unfair things that happen to us. However, God grants these things and uses them to form our hearts in a way that we will transcend this dying world and find our true happiness in the world to come.

As such, we are constantly kicking against the goads. We kick and scream, struggle and endeavor to resist God's guidance and the control He exercises over our lives for our own good. However, we have some sort of fantasy idea of God's will for our lives which only lines up with our notion that it is all about the pursuit of happiness.

It is interesting to take note of the fact that the next thing Jesus talks about are oaths—vows. When we make an oath to God, the Bible tells us He hates those who break them as we will see next. It is better that we just show an integrity towards what we speak. Just because we change our mind, it is irreverent and a willful blindness to spiritual reality to not consider we involved God and promised Him. Or that we must account to Him for every oath we make. Again, the whole spiritual aspect doesn't seem real or significant. Promises to God are the most often broken promises and the ones we have the least concern over breaking. This shows how little the spiritual is real to us.

Jesus also warns us away from using God and His name as a weight in order to get people to believe us. It is irreverent, and does not give God the respect due Him. It is a form of using God to get what we want. It is no different than using His laws to serve self and not what they were meant to be used for—that is to serve God and others.

This issue reminds me of my sister. When in a heated argument about facts, and she runs out of facts to support her opinion, she would always rely on this one thing to win the debate. "I read it in a book that was written by a Nobel prize winning scientist, oh and you think you know better than him?" I dreaded when she would whip that one out, because it's a no win situation. You are not arguing with her anymore, you are telling Albert Einstein that he is wrong and stupid. You become an arrogant, unreasonable, know-it-all who is never wrong. . . . . End of argument! Jesus didn't like to be used that way any more than we like someone using Him that way against us:

NIV Lk 12:13 *Someone in the crowd said to him, "Teacher, tell my brother to divide the inheritance with me."*
NIV Lk 12:14 *Jesus replied, "Man, who appointed me a judge or an arbiter between you?"*

Jesus is adamant about the use of God's name in vain; there is a law against it. To include Him or use Him as weight or clout to dominate others or to force them to trust you, even to put people in a position where they cannot question you because it would be tantamount to accusing God, well, let's just say it is not something you want to answer to when you finally face Him. You cannot really behold God as real, fully appreciating who you are trifling with and, at the same time, treat His name in this fashion.

Oaths

NIV Mt 5:33 *"Again, you have heard that it was said to the people long ago, 'Do not break your oath, but keep the oaths you have made to the Lord.'*
NIV Mt 5:34 *But I tell you, Do not swear at all: either by heaven, for it is God's throne;*
NIV Mt 5:35 *or by the earth, for it is his footstool; or by Jerusalem, for it is the city of the Great King.*
NIV Mt 5:36 *And do not swear by your head, for you cannot make even one hair white or black.*
NIV Mt 5:37 *Simply let your 'Yes' be 'Yes,' and your 'No,' 'No'; anything beyond this comes from the evil one.*

An Eye for an Eye

NIV Mt 5:38 *"You have heard that it was said, 'Eye for eye, and tooth for tooth.'*
NIV Mt 5:39 *But I tell you, Do not resist an evil person. If someone strikes you on the right cheek, turn to him the other also.*
NIV Mt 5:40 *And if someone wants to sue you and take your tunic, let him have your cloak as well.*
NIV Mt 5:41 *If someone forces you to go one mile, go with him two miles.*
NIV Mt 5:42 *Give to the one who asks you, and do not turn away from the one who wants to borrow from you.*

What Jesus teaches us in saying, "an eye for an eye," is tied to what He teaches about love for your enemies, judging others, and forgiveness. In keeping those teachings, it is certain that we will take it on the chin (as it were). We will potentially lose control, be taken advantage of, and be cheated out of our fair share. As a result, we will become like David; we will experientially condition ourselves into letting God rule and be in charge of what is right.

Although not all of us will go through the great tribulation, all of us will go through our own personal tribulations. There is a reason for this. It is the same reason that the Israelites were destined to go through 400 years of forced servitude (slavery). That reason was covered earlier. However, it is because of the defect in the heart of man. It takes hard and consistent experiential conditioning to change the heart and spirit of the non-spiritual man.

God wanted to have a people for Himself that He could bless with eternal life, so He needed to take measures in order for those people to learn to serve something other than themselves. Forced servitude leads to an ability to serve something other than self. God wants to give us (the objects of His mercy) the ability to serve Him voluntarily out of love and out of a desire to be in union with Him. Bringing us through personal tribulations while keeping the way Jesus teaches, our life experiences will turn our hearts voluntarily, just as forced servitude was meant to turn the hearts of the Israelites.

Here is something even the general Christian population doesn't know or take seriously: The world was judged once with a flood, resulting in the Lord's promise to never wipe out mankind again with a flood. However, from the beginning of our second chance through the lineage of Noah, mankind has proven themselves unchanged and continued to pursue the things they did before the flood. Soon after, judgments came which toppled the tower of Babel and scattered the people around the face of the earth, dividing it up into 70 nations with 70 different languages. Nevertheless, man continued to show his defiance towards subordinating under God.

One man, Nimrod, defied the commands of God and, through the force of an army he had gathered, conquered and took a neighboring land, settling where he was commanded not to. That land was one of the other of the seventy nations which God divided up among the descendants of Noah. He continued against the commands of God, building great cities so that he could lord over men for his own power (some of these ancient cities exist today). Babylon was the first city he built in defiance to God. When he defied the Lord and was not killed, the people made him king over all the earth, because he swore to protect them from Yahweh so they could do as they pleased without repercussions from God.

In the Bible, he was also called "the Assyrian," which is the first area he defied God by conquering and taking as his own. Nimrod is the antichrist, and the one who will rise up from the dead, out of the Abyss, to rule during the great tribulation. The antichrist means (among other things) another christ; he is not just the opposite of the Christ of God, but the "other savior." The Christ of God comes down from Heaven to die as a sacrifice for our sins and reconcile us to God, saving us from destruction. The antichrist rises up from the Abyss, boasting to save us from God and His wrath so that we are free to do as we will, living independent from God. In the end, these are our two choices. They will not be unclear.

It was then, when all the people of the earth made Nimrod king over them so they could do as they pleased (in defiance of God) with Nimrod's protection, that God judged the world a second time. The first time was with water, but this time is with fire. All the earth, its inhabitants (alive and dead) and the physical universe will be thrown into the eternal lake of fire. The lake already exists for this purpose but is, however, empty, awaiting the last day when all will be judged. This is with the exception of the antichrist and his false prophet. After their time during the great tribulation, they will be thrown alive into the lake of fire upon Jesus' victory at the battle of Armageddon. They will solely occupy the lake of fire until the last day of the natural earth 1000 years later. When that time comes, all that is destined to be destroyed will also finally be thrown into this eternal fire with them.

God will go further in this judgment than He did with the flood, in which He allowed the earth to flourish once again. With the judgment of fire, everything will be destroyed in its entirety. Likewise, no natural men will survive. Even Hades will be emptied, which is the place for the unclothed souls (the dead) who formerly walked the earth. Its inhabitants will be clothed once again with a body, so they can face final judgment. Having been emptied and its purpose having expired, Hades, too, will be thrown into the lake of fire. The people, having been resurrected, will be judged as fit to go on and live in the world to come as celestial humans for eternity, or fit to be thrown alive into the lake of fire and thus suffer a second death or disembodiment of the soul.

The decision and judgment has already been made, even within a few generations of those who survived the flood. It is irreversible! It is a judgment that is being implemented in stages, because God promised

Noah that He would not destroy all humanity as He did in the flood. The physical universe will perish, but before it does, God will take for Himself many natural humans who He will transform into celestial humans through a rebirth—being born again of a different nature. These survivors of the natural universe will live on as new creations for eternity in the spiritual realm. God indeed will keep His promise to Noah.

Here is the thing we as humans and Christians need to understand: the gavel went down and judgment has begun! The conclusion of the judgment has not yet come; nevertheless, the judgment process has already begun. As a result, ever since that gavel went down and the judgment started to take effect, living life on earth has stopped being about living a life of finding contentment. Life on earth is no longer the point. It is about living in a manner that will qualify you for a pardon, escaping this world which is doomed for destruction. It is in the world to come that we will find contentment. The people of this world need to change their whole reason for living if they wish to survive death, disembodiment of their soul, and the destruction of the natural universe. We need to let the greedy and the God haters have this world, and instead live for the world to come. James sums this up very well.

NIV Jas 1:9 The brother in humble circumstances ought to take pride in his high position.

NIV Jas 1:10 But the one who is rich should take pride in his low position, because he will pass away like a wild flower.

NIV Jas 1:11 For the sun rises with scorching heat and withers the plant; its blossom falls and its beauty is destroyed. In the same way, the rich man will fade away even while he goes about his business.

"The sun rises," is the light of God dawning on the earth bringing with it its final judgment. James is saying that even while the rich and powerful are working their way up the latter of success and establishing a way for themselves, the bottom is dropping out from underneath them. While their empire is growing, the world has begun the process of its doom. It is a sinking ship they are building their empire on. He goes on to say to the ones oppressed by them:

NIV Jas 1:12 *Blessed is the man who perseveres under trial, <u>because when he has stood the test</u>, he will receive the crown of life that God has promised to those who love him.*

NIV Jas 5:1 *Now listen, you rich people, weep and wail because of the misery that is coming upon you.*
NIV Jas 5:2 *Your wealth has rotted, and moths have eaten your clothes.*
NIV Jas 5:3 *Your gold and silver are corroded. Their corrosion will testify against you and eat your flesh like fire. You have hoarded wealth in the last days.*
NIV Jas 5:4 *Look! The wages you failed to pay the workmen who mowed your fields are crying out against you. The cries of the harvesters have reached the ears of the Lord Almighty.*
NIV Jas 5:5 *You have lived on earth in luxury and self-indulgence. You have fattened yourselves in the day of slaughter.*
NIV Jas 5:6 *You have condemned and murdered innocent men, who were not opposing you.*

As a part of the judgment of the earth and the people who wanted to live independent from God, God gave the world over to that king Nimrod. God released a power and authority to him who is the antichrist. He is the white horse whose rider has a crown and a bow and who was bent on conquest, God released on the earth (Rev 6:2). The white horse is the power, the crown is the authority, and the rider is the antichrist. God has judged the world to be destroyed and has given it over, for a time, to those who would defy God and enslave the people for their own wealth. It was what the people wanted when they made Nimrod king over them. However, God is using their lust for power and domination as a way to purify with fire the objects of His mercies.

Our personal tribulations in the world are meant to make us pure and open up our hearts so that we can learn to serve God. This is why Jesus instructs us not to fight back and not hate those who persecute us and sin against us. Like King David with the man throwing stones at him, God is allowing our personal tribulations to humble us so that we might be made right for salvation. The shallow-minded see obstacles, setbacks, and injustices as something that is delaying or stealing away their happiness in this world. However, Jesus is teaching us, the spiritually-minded, to understand the same challenges as from a good God, on our side, trying to mold our hearts so that He might bless us eternally.

The power and authority of the four horsemen was released.

Many believe this is something that will be released during the end times. But the story Revelation tells starts at the beginning. That beginning was the new beginning after the flood, when the 8 survivors of it disembarked the ark.

It is easily verified by recognizing that all of the curses of the four horsemen are in the world today, and they have been since a few generations after the flood. Empirical domination, enslavement, and death by violence, starvation (famine), disease, natural disasters, and wild animals has been occurring since shortly after the flood. In addition, in the Old Testament, when God would pronounce judgment on a city or a people, He would call the means of their destruction His four winds of destruction. These are: death by war/sword, wild animals, famine, and nature (both disease and natural disasters). There are multiple occasions in the Old Testament when He makes reference to them.

At one point, Jesus told the crowds that they did not understand His miracles:

GNT Jn 6:26 Jesus answered, "I am telling you the truth: you are looking for me because you ate the bread and had all you wanted, not because you understood my miracles.

Again, Jesus implores the people to believe Him and His identity because of the miracles.

NIV Jn 10:37 Do not believe me unless I do what my Father does.
NIV Jn 10:38 But if I do it, even though you do not believe me, believe the miracles, that you may know and understand that the Father is in me, and I in the Father."

It is clear that we are to understand something important about Him because of the miracles. For the most part we are supposed to identify Him as the Messiah, the Savior of the world, because of the miracles. How do His miracles show us this? Taking a look at the kinds of miracles He did should certainly tell us.

There was a power and authority released in the earth, which included the authority of the four horsemen and their power—the four winds of destruction. It was released as a part of the final judgment on the earth. Then and now, the four horsemen and the winds of destruction are the highest authority in the earth, except for God Himself.

One look at the types of miracles Jesus performed, and we should see that He possessed an authority and power that was above that of the four horsemen. They could kill and starve through famine. Jesus fed the masses from nothing, and promised that whoever came to Him would never go hungry or be thirsty. They have the power to prematurely bring to an end an ongoing 25% of the lives of the people on the earth. Jesus raised people from the dead. They have the power of nature/natural catastrophes to destroy and take lives, which includes disease. Jesus rebuked the storms, walked on the water, and He also healed the sick.

What we are supposed to understand by His miracles is that Jesus has an authority and a power above that which has been released in the earth as judgment. His Father gave it to Him. This tells us that He is our only hope—our way out, He is the Messiah, the Savior of the world, the One who can save us from the destruction that has been pronounced and released over the earth and its people. Through Him, we can receive a pardon and escape the judgment that began its process a few generations after the flood and, when finished, will destroy the entire universe and everything in it.

Amp Ro 9:21 *Has the potter no right over the clay, to make out of the same mass (lump) one vessel for beauty and distinction and honorable use, and another for menial or ignoble and dishonorable use?* *Amp Ro 9:22* *What if God, although fully intending to show [the awfulness of] His wrath and to make known His power and authority, has tolerated with much patience the vessels (objects) of [His] anger which are ripe for destruction?* *Amp Ro 9:23* *And [what if] He thus purposes to make known and show the wealth of His glory in [dealing with] the vessels (objects) of His mercy which He has prepared beforehand for glory,* *Amp Ro 9:24* *Even including ourselves whom He has called, not only from among the Jews but also from among the Gentiles (heathen)?*

Why has God released something so terrible? Why give someone the power to be king over the whole world, conquer every nation, enslave the people, and allow the four winds of destruction to enforce their power? The reason is: the people of the earth are condemned along with the natural universe. He is giving the greedy and the rebellious the authority and power to take it, those who He deems unredeemable, because they are bent on being a law unto themselves, and living in their own power. It is their moment to shine. In doing so, they oppress and enslave the rest. Those who they oppress have their last chance to let themselves be humbled. They have the force of the wicked to help them do so.

In doing so, the humble in heart gain an ability to serve something other than themselves. They learn to submit to God. By using the evil in this world to take your piece of the pie, you are showing yourself to be worthy of destruction. By being humble, and not rising up to take the brass ring, you are putting your hope in the world to come, and not in this world. Our personal tribulations and the great tribulation are meant to purify and show our hearts for what they are and what they choose.

Amp Da 11:33 *And they who are wise and understanding among the people shall instruct many and make them understand, though some [of them and their followers] shall fall by the sword and flame, by captivity and plunder, for many days.*

Amp Da 11:34 *Now when they fall, they shall receive a little help. Many shall join themselves to them with flatteries and hypocrisies.*

Amp Da 11:35 *And some of those who are wise, prudent, and understanding shall be weakened and fall, [thus, then, the insincere among the people will lose courage and become deserters. It will be a test] to refine, to purify, and to make those among [God's people] white* (pure), *even to the time of the end, because it is yet for the time [God] appointed.*

Our personal tribulations are meant to purify us and expose and establish us as ones who will be lovers of self, looking out for number one, or lovers of God, in service to Him no matter what that means to us. Again, as ones who want to submit under the Christ and be saved from ourselves and our own sins, or be saved by the antichrist who would protect us from Yahweh so we can do as we will. It all comes down to this.

Love for Enemies

NIV Mt 5:43 *"You have heard that it was said, 'Love your neighbor and hate your enemy.'*

NIV Mt 5:44 *But I tell you: Love your enemies and pray for those who persecute you,*

NIV Mt 5:45 *that you may be sons of your Father in heaven. He causes his sun to rise on the evil and the good, and sends rain on the righteous and the unrighteous.*

NIV Mt 5:46 *If you love those who love you, what reward will you get? Are not even the tax collectors doing that?*

NIV Mt 5:47 *And if you greet only your brothers, what are you doing more than others? Do not even pagans do that?*

NIV Mt 5:48 *Be perfect, therefore, as your heavenly Father is perfect.*

Giving to the Needy

NIV Mt 6:1 *"Be careful not to do your 'acts of righteousness' before men, to be seen by them. If you do, you will have no reward from your Father in heaven.*

NIV Mt 6:2 *"So when you give to the needy, do not announce it with trumpets, as the hypocrites do in the synagogues and on the streets, to be honored by men. I tell you the truth, they have received their reward in full.*

NIV Mt 6:3 *But when you give to the needy, do not let your left hand know what your right hand is doing,*

NIV Mt 6:4 *so that your giving may be in secret. Then your Father, who sees what is done in secret, will reward you.*

These verses have the same message as: you reap what you sow and invest in the world to come . . .

Prayer

NIV Mt 6:5 *"And when you pray, do not be like the hypocrites, for they love to pray standing in the synagogues and on the street corners to be seen by men. I tell you the truth, they have received their reward in full.*

NIV Mt 6:6 *But when you pray, go into your room, close the door and pray to your Father, who is unseen. Then your Father, who sees what is done in secret, will reward you.*

NIV Mt 6:7 *And when you pray, do not keep on babbling like pagans, for they think they will be heard because of their many words.*

NIV Mt 6:8 *Do not be like them, for your Father knows what you need before you ask him.*

We learned early on in our ministry the lesson in the verses above. Quite often when we would have ministry needs or personal needs we would pray about them daily, keeping our prayers constantly before God. Then, we began to notice something . . . we were hearing from God less and less. Then we finally got the message; we were so busy talking and requesting from God that we never gave Him time to speak. And our focus was not to find out what He was saying, but to tell Him what we needed/desired. We found the Lord to be patient. If it was not what He wanted us to do for Him or the concern He wanted to be our focus, He would get silent, and let us go on and on about what we needed and how bad we needed it and why it was the solution for what our needs were.

As a group, one day we understood God's silence and finally figured out that we were talking to Him about things He didn't want to talk about—things that He was going to take care of in His way, in His time, and not ours. So when we prayed, we decided His silence meant that we hadn't hit the subject matter that He was concerned about for that day. From that day forth, we decided to go to God with an objective heart, wanting to know His agenda, His concerns, and what His Holy Spirit wanted us to focus on for that day. Then we trusted Him with the rest. If we had burning needs that had us in fear, we would make those fears known, but drop it, knowing that God knew better than us what needed to transpire in every situation. We decided from then on out that our prayer time should primarily be about finding out what He wanted us to be concerned with and what He wanted us to accomplish. It was no longer a time to give Him a laundry list of all of the things we wanted Him to perform for us so that we could help Him.

NIV Mt 6:9 *"This, then, is how you should pray: " 'Our Father in heaven, hallowed be your name,*
NIV Mt 6:10 *your kingdom come, your will be done on earth as it is in heaven.*
NIV Mt 6:11 *Give us today our daily bread.*
NIV Mt 6:12 *Forgive us our debts, as we also have forgiven our debtors.*

NIV Mt 6:13 *And lead us not into temptation, but deliver us from the evil one.'*

NIV Mt 6:14 *For if you forgive men when they sin against you, your heavenly Father will also forgive you.*

NIV Mt 6:15 *But if you do not forgive men their sins, your Father will not forgive your sins.*

Fasting

NIV Mt 6:16 *"When you fast, do not look somber as the hypocrites do, for they disfigure their faces to show men they are fasting. I tell you the truth, they have received their reward in full.*

NIV Mt 6:17 *But when you fast, put oil on your head and wash your face,*

NIV Mt 6:18 *so that it will not be obvious to men that you are fasting, but only to your Father, who is unseen; and your Father, who sees what is done in secret, will reward you.*

The message in these above verses was already covered when we reviewed the verse that teaches you reap what you sow (Gal 6:8). It is really important to understand that if, in our heart of hearts, we do an act expecting to reap a benefit in this world, then that is exactly where our efforts will be applied. So if, in our hearts, we want men to recognize how pious we are, then the seeds we plant with our prayers will be planted in the superficial world, and not in the spiritual world. Now, whether those seeds we plant in the world bear fruit is another story. Men may still not see us as pious as we wish.

It's just like a farmer. He may put many seeds in the ground; however, not all of them will grow and bear fruit. However, wherever we invest, that's where we will reap a harvest. If a farmer has two fields it would be ridiculous for him to plant seeds in one of them and expect the plants to grow in another. Do things to receive praises from men, and that is exactly the ground your seed will be planted. Do things to honor your Father in Heaven, and that is exactly the ground your seeds will be planted. Again, it's like shooting a gun. The bullet comes out of the gun and goes in the direction that you have pointed it. It's not possible for the bullet to come out of the gun and go in a different direction.

Jesus is saying that when you are deliberate in sowing your seeds in the world to come, our Father in Heaven will most certainly make sure you reap a harvest of righteousness in the spiritual realm. The following verses (Treasures in Heaven) reiterate this point, making it clear. If we are to be spiritual people, we need to invest in the world to come, which is in the spirit realm, forgetting about this present world which is doomed to destruction.

Treasures in Heaven

NIV Mt 6:19 *"Do not store up for yourselves treasures on earth, where moth and rust destroy, and where thieves break in and steal.*
NIV Mt 6:20 *But store up for yourselves treasures in heaven, where moth and rust do not destroy, and where thieves do not break in and steal.*
NIV Mt 6:21 *For where your treasure is, there your heart will be also.*

It is very interesting to take note that when people recite this verse, they quite often reverse it. Some will say where your heart is, there also is your treasure. It's kind of like the verse that says the love of money is the root of all evil. However, many people quote it as saying money is the root of all evil.

What you desire, what you value, and what you seek after, your spirit bends and reaches out towards. It becomes a primary focus of your heart, and you think of all things in light of what you treasure. For example, if one of the most important things in your life is to party and meet people of the opposite sex, then you will spend your whole work week waiting and anticipating for Friday to come. You will spend a great deal of the money you made not just on Friday night itself, but everything that makes it a better experience. Like clothes and shoes and a nice car and haircuts and so on. Often your vocation/work becomes something to contend with and in the way of Friday night coming. If this is what is important to you, this will be your focus, this is what you will treasure. This is what will take priority, and everything about it is what you will occupy your heart with for the majority of the time. We love the created more than the Creator, who made all these things for our joy.

Imagine having a wife or husband or friend that loves all the gifts we give them and the things we do to make their life joyful more than they love us. In fact, consider if they outright ignored you waiting only for the next thing you would give them, accordingly, they would show love for the things you give them but not for you. In the world they call that "what have you done for me lately" love. In truth, once it gets past a certain level, it is idolatry and it makes the Scripture in Romans true:

NLT Ro 1:18 But God shows his anger from heaven against all sinful, wicked people who push the truth away from themselves.

NLT Ro 1:19 For the truth about God is known to them instinctively. God has put this knowledge in their hearts.

NLT Ro 1:20 From the time the world was created, people have seen the earth and sky and all that God made. They can clearly see his invisible qualities—his eternal power and divine nature (by observing nature). *So they have no excuse whatsoever for not knowing God.*

NLT Ro 1:21 Yes, they knew God, but they wouldn't worship him as God or even give him thanks. And they began to think up foolish ideas of what God was like. The result was that their minds became dark and confused.

NLT Ro 1:22 Claiming to be wise, they became utter fools instead.

NLT Ro 1:23 And instead of worshiping the glorious, ever-living God, they worshiped idols made to look like mere people, or birds and animals and snakes.

NLT Ro 1:24 So God let them go ahead and do whatever shameful things their hearts desired. As a result, they did vile and degrading things with each other's bodies.

NLT Ro 1:25 Instead of believing what they knew was the truth about God, they deliberately chose to believe lies. So they worshiped the things God made but not the Creator himself, who is to be praised forever. Amen.

NLT Ro 1:26 *That is why God abandoned them to their shameful desires. Even the women turned against the natural way to have sex and instead indulged in sex with each other.*

NLT Ro 1:27 *And the men, instead of having normal sexual relationships with women, burned with lust for each other. Men did shameful things with other men and, as a result, suffered within themselves the penalty they so richly deserved.*

NLT Ro 1:28 *When they refused to acknowledge God, he abandoned them to their evil minds and let them do things that should never be done.*

NLT Ro 1:29 *Their lives became full of every kind of wickedness, sin, greed, hate, envy, murder, fighting, deception, malicious behavior, and gossip.*

NLT Ro 1:30 *They are backstabbers, haters of God, insolent, proud, and boastful. They are forever inventing new ways of sinning and are disobedient to their parents.*

NLT Ro 1:31 *They refuse to understand, break their promises, and are heartless and unforgiving.*

NLT Ro 1:32 *They are fully aware of God's death penalty for those who do these things, yet they go right ahead and do them anyway. And, worse yet, they encourage others to do them, too.*

This is just like when Jesus told us that it's not what you put into the mouth and eat that defiles the body, but what comes out of your lips from within your heart. Likewise, He tells us, below, that the eyes reflect the qualities of our soul—our inner heart.

NIV Mt 6:22 *"The eye is the lamp of the body. If your eyes are good, your whole body will be full of light.*

NIV Mt 6:23 *But if your eyes are bad, your whole body will be full of darkness. If then the light within you is darkness, how great is that darkness!*

NIV Mt 6:24 *"No one can serve two masters. Either he will hate the one and love the other, or he will be devoted to the one and despise the other. You cannot serve both God and Money.*

Do Not Worry

^{NIV Mt 6:25} *"Therefore I tell you, do not worry about your life, what you will eat or drink; or about your body, what you will wear. Is not life more important than food, and the body more important than clothes?*

^{NIV Mt 6:26} *Look at the birds of the air; they do not sow or reap or store away in barns, and yet your heavenly Father feeds them. Are you not much more valuable than they?*

^{NIV Mt 6:27} *Who of you by worrying can add a single hour to his life?*

^{NIV Mt 6:28} *"And why do you worry about clothes? See how the lilies of the field grow. They do not labor or spin.*

^{NIV Mt 6:29} *Yet I tell you that not even Solomon in all his splendor was dressed like one of these.*

^{NIV Mt 6:30} *If that is how God clothes the grass of the field, which is here today and tomorrow is thrown into the fire, will he not much more clothe you, O you of little faith?*

^{NIV Mt 6:31} *So do not worry, saying, 'What shall we eat?' or 'What shall we drink?' or 'What shall we wear?'*

^{NIV Mt 6:32} *For the pagans run after all these things, and your heavenly Father knows that you need them.*

^{NIV Mt 6:33} *But seek first his kingdom and his righteousness, and all these things will be given to you as well.*

^{NIV Mt 6:34} *Therefore do not worry about tomorrow, for tomorrow will worry about itself. Each day has enough trouble of its own.*

It was pointed out earlier in the study that each spirit and its energy has a motive that is unique to the spirit. The example of the spirit of fear was given. People who possess the spirit of fear are often looked at as being passive and victims. In reality, the motive of the spirit of fear is to control. Those who possess the spirit of fear are not victims but perpetrators, imposing massive spiritual force through their anxieties in an effort to will things to turn out as they see fit. As such, it is easy to understand why Jesus would instruct us to not worry about the future or how things are going to turn out. In doing so, we have a heart and will to control things and we take control away from God.

The other interesting thing to note about fear, in a positive context, is that to fear is to worship. To fear, in this context, means to yield your will to the will of another's. For example, you take all of your hard earned money from the bank and someone with a gun comes along threatening your life if you don't give him the money. Out of fear, you hand the money over to him. Your will was to take that money and use it to buy yourself a car. His will was to take that money from you and spend it on his pleasure. Out of fear, you yielded your will to his and gave him your money.

It is the same with God. One of the greatest ways we can worship Him is to fear Him, the Bible tells us. That does not mean we dread Him and are afraid of Him. What it means is that we yield our will to the will of God, and, in this way, it is true worship to God. Fear (yielding our will to His) is worship. Many of the psalms teach us a concept that a great deal of people cannot relate to because of their ideas about fear.

That concept is this: when we fear God in this fashion by yielding our will to His and living in dependency upon His control, we do not feel dread and loneliness and unprotectedness. Rather, we experience a closeness to God that is indescribable—a sense of joy, safety, and an intimate love with God. Fear, in its proper usage, brings safety, comfort, and peace to our soul, not like the dread and anxiety that comes from fearing the created instead of the Creator. Likewise, when we let go of control of our lives, stop having a fear of how it will turn out, and, instead, worship God (the Creator who gives us all good things) in thanksgiving for all of the gifts and sustenance He provides us with, then we are living in the fear of God and He remains in our hearts, God in control.

Judging Others

NIV Mt 7:1 *"Do not judge, or you too will be judged.*

NIV Mt 7:2 *For in the same way you judge others, you will be judged, and with the measure you use, it will be measured to you.*

NIV Mt 7:3 *"Why do you look at the speck of sawdust in your brother's eye and pay no attention to the plank in your own eye?*

NIV Mt 7:4 *How can you say to your brother, 'Let me take the speck out of your eye,' when all the time there is a plank in your own eye?*

NIV Mt 7:5 *You hypocrite, first take the plank out of your own eye, and then you will see clearly to remove the speck from your brother's eye.*

An interesting note here is that in both this occasion and the parable about forgiveness, we are made to be the bad guy. In the one about forgiveness, the man owed his master 10,000 talents (millions of dollars) and got forgiveness, but he was only owed 100 denarius (a few months wages), which he did not forgive. In this case, the wrongdoer merely has a speck in his eye, whereas you who are wronged have a plank of wood in your eye. This begs the question: Why is it that we owe this huge debt and have this huge obstruction in our eye when the wrongdoers in our lives have merely a fraction of debt owed to us and have just a minute obstruction concerning how they see us?

The reason behind this is that the huge debt is the accumulated debt we owe God during a lifetime of sinning. This is a much greater debt than that of someone who may have injured us on a few occasions. It is the same with the plank in our eye. One's dim view of us may allow him to objectify us and take advantage of us in some ways. However, our entire worldview not only objectifies God, but ignores His presence and strips Him of all control and due respect (in our estimation).

NIV Mt 7:6 *"Do not give dogs what is sacred; do not throw your pearls to pigs. If you do, they may trample them under their feet, and then turn and tear you to pieces.*

Here is another noteworthy observation. Verse 6 (above) is easily interpreted on its own merit. However, it's a rather strange saying for Jesus to speak right after talking about judging. Everything spoken about in the beatitudes flows. The next saying always follows the previous one. That being the case, one has to wonder why this is inserted as a part of the sayings about judging.

In counseling people who have been abused or taken advantage of by authority figures or loved ones, one of the most important priorities that will bring healing and peace into the soul of the victim is for them to forgive those who have harmed them. They have to let go of their judgments, hatred, desire for the other party to see and admit how they have wronged them, and their need for retribution. It is only after they release these people from their debt, forgive them, and no longer judge them that the healing begins.

This is a very commonly understood concept in the Christian community. Let's say, for example, one has a physically and emotionally abusive spouse. Many Christians believe that if they forgive them and stop judging them in a condemning, way it means that they have to invite that person back into their lives. We try to help people understand that you can forgive someone and let go of your judgments, but that doesn't mean you need to invite the abuse back into your life. Many people have trouble with this idea; they think to do so is unforgiveness.

Given that this saying about throwing pearls before pigs is spoken right after we are admonished to forgive and to not judge tells us the same thing. Although Jesus instructs us to forgive and stop judging harshly those who have harmed us, He is balancing these instructions by saying that, in going forward, it is not prudent to put yourself in a position for the same people to have opportunity to take advantage of you and bring harm to you all over again. In other words, you can remove yourself from abusive situations while having a forgiving heart instead of judging and wanting retribution.

Jesus is saying that it is better to resolve the situation by removing yourself from it, than to fight for your rights and take what is yours or force people to treat you right by threat of retribution. This makes us people of peace, who defuse and disarm situations instead of escalating them. Again, this is why God, who hates divorce, instructs the believer to let their spouse leave rather than fight, argue, and force them to stay. This is because, it goes on to say, "We are people of peace."

If people do not accept us for the truth we bring them, the Lord instructs us not to cram it down their throats and force them to comply, but to turn away from them and to shake the very dust of their town off of our feet and walk away. To shake the dust off of our feet is to let it go and forget their hostility by moving on. Do not continue to talk about it and go over it in your mind until you upset yourself, or continue to bring it back to them until they admit that how they have wronged you. Why? Because we are people of peace, we are to disarm and defuse, not escalate. We remove ourselves from situations which go nowhere instead of fighting for our rights and for people to admit that they were wrong. To do otherwise is like trying to convince the Devil he is a liar when he continues to deny. He knows it's true; he is deciding to believe his lies.

It is necessary to temper this teaching by pointing out that there are times when the Lord asks us to stay in situations that have a negative effect on us. In these occasions, we do not walk away from them, but remain obedient to the Holy Spirit by not trying to escape until we are released. Again, the Lord has His own purposes for what we go through in our lives. After all, we are to be His body, living out His Spirit urgings which come from His wisdom, reasons, and will.

Ask, Seek, Knock

NIV Mt 7:7 *"Ask and it will be given to you; seek and you will find; knock and the door will be opened to you.*

NIV Mt 7:8 *For everyone who asks receives; he who seeks finds; and to him who knocks, the door will be opened.*

NIV Mt 7:9 *"Which of you, if his son asks for bread, will give him a stone?*

NIV Mt 7:10 *Or if he asks for a fish, will give him a snake?*

NIV Mt 7:11 *If you, then, though you are evil, know how to give good gifts to your children, how much more will your Father in heaven give good gifts to those who ask him!*

NIV Mt 7:12 *So in everything, do to others what you would have them do to you, for this sums up the Law and the Prophets.*

Again, we have a concluding statement that is seemingly not in line with its accompanied teaching. But if you take time to see how they complement each other, what can be ascertained out of the concluding statement is this: In this way, the Father is responsive to us in a nurturing way and that we would want other people to respect us in the same way, then we too should treat others this way. It's similar to the statement, "Be perfect, therefore, as your heavenly Father is perfect" (MT 5:48). Or " Treat others the same way you want them to treat you" (LK 6:31). God sets the bar, or the example, of how we are to respect, nurture, and relate to each other.

He teaches us in these very same beatitudes that not only are we supposed to love our neighbors as our very own selves, but that we are to love our enemies in the same way. In this case, when using the word "love," its meaning is to nurture, care for, and to promote life. Likewise, when the Bible talks about hate, it's not referring to an emotion, but an action. In other words, to hate is to not nurture and not promote life or care for an individual, the opposite of love.

The Narrow and Wide Gates

NIV Mt 7:13 *"Enter through the narrow gate. For wide is the gate and broad is the road that leads to destruction, and many enter through it.*

NIV Mt 7:14 *But small is the gate and narrow the road that leads to life, and only a few find it.*

It is said around the world that there are many paths to travel, but they all lead to the top of the mountain. Jesus is categorically denying this misnomer. He is saying, to become a celestial being (so as to avoid destruction), there is only one way. That one way does not have a lot of latitude. To travel that path requires one to be humble, submitted, and, with total self-distrust, rely on something outside of themselves, Jesus.

A Tree and Its Fruit

NIV Mt 7:15 *"Watch out for false prophets. They come to you in sheep's clothing, but inwardly they are ferocious wolves.*

NIV Mt 7:16 *By their fruit you will recognize them. Do people pick grapes from thornbushes, or figs from thistles?*

NIV Mt 7:17 *Likewise every good tree bears good fruit, but a bad tree bears bad fruit.*

NIV Mt 7:18 *A good tree cannot bear bad fruit, and a bad tree cannot bear good fruit.*

NIV Mt 7:19 *Every tree that does not bear good fruit is cut down and thrown into the fire.*

NIV Mt 7:20 *Thus, by their fruit you will recognize them.*

NIV Mt 7:21 *"Not everyone who says to me, 'Lord, Lord,' will enter the kingdom of heaven, but only he who does the will of my Father who is in heaven.*

NIV Mt 7:22 *Many will say to me on that day, 'Lord, Lord, did we not prophesy in your name, and in your name drive out demons and perform many miracles?'*

NIV Mt 7:23 *Then I will tell them plainly, 'I never knew you. Away from me, you evildoers!'*

The Wise and Foolish Builders

NIV Mt 7:24 *"Therefore everyone who hears these words of mine and puts them into practice is like a wise man who built his house on the rock.*

NIV Mt 7:25 *The rain came down, the streams rose, and the winds blew and beat against that house; yet it did not fall, because it had its foundation on the rock.*

NIV Mt 7:26 *But everyone who hears these words of mine and does not put them into practice is like a foolish man who built his house on sand.*

NIV Mt 7:27 *The rain came down, the streams rose, and the winds blew and beat against that house, and it fell with a great crash."*

NIV Mt 7:28 When Jesus had finished saying these things, the crowds were amazed at his teaching,

NIV Mt 7:29 because he taught as one who had authority, and not as their teachers of the law.

It was not the intentions of the authors to give commentary on all the beatitudes spoken by Jesus. The intention was to help open spiritual eyes to see the deeper wisdom and purposes of His teachings. Encrypted in the sayings of Jesus, which seemingly are rules to live by, is the wisdom of true enlightenment. His sayings are much more than rules to keep, but by exploring and understanding them, we can learn to function and view life as spiritual men and women. We can learn to view our lives from a totally different perspective. That is the perspective of a spiritually orientated human—a celestial human.

Unlike any other saint or sage who walked the face of the earth, Jesus, by His Spirit that carries His words which when we ingest and understand them, we become born again. The same soul, now enlightened by His Spirit words, is given a new embodiment, trading the physical/mortal body doomed for death (as all the natural world), for a new and indestructible celestial body. By His words, the universe was created and came to be, and by His words, we become born again as spirit beings, thus given a way out of a lost and dying world. A world under a sentence of eternal destruction. The non-canonical Gospel of Thomas, which lists out the sayings of Jesus, begins with this:

These are the hidden words that the living Jesus spoke,

and that Didymos Judas Thomas wrote down.

Saying one:
And He (Jesus) *said, "Whoever finds the meaning of these words will not taste death."*

To the perishing world, this is considered foolishness, nevertheless, it is a serious thing. The Bible tells us that when we come into union with Christ, worshiping Him in Spirit and in truth—having taken on this wisdom from Heaven—we are no longer what Paul calls, "mere men" (1Cor 3:3-4). We have become what we term, "celestial humans," or children of God, brothers of Jesus—who is the first born Son of many. Our nature changes to angelic-type beings whose natural habitat is in the spiritual realm, and no longer the natural universe.

As such, we will rule the natural earth and the natural humans on it with Jesus from the supernatural city, the New Jerusalem, when He comes into His Kingdom. When that predetermined time comes to a close, the entire natural universe will suddenly end with a crash; every element will melt as it is thrown into the lake of fire. Those living on the earth at that time will suddenly find themselves naked—unclothed, without an embodiment to give expression to their soul. For everything made of natural matter will be destroyed in the lake of fire.

Amp 2Pe 3:10 But the day of the Lord will come like a thief, and then the heavens will vanish (pass away) with a thunderous crash, and the [material] elements [of the universe] will be dissolved with fire, and the earth and the works that are upon it will be burned up.

All of humanity, including those who were already dead from Adam forward, will be resurrected and given a new body to clothe their soul with.

This resurrection also includes those who suddenly perished on the last day and became disembodied souls when their natural bodies perished. They all will be clothed once again with a body in order to face God and be judged. They will be either judged worthy to continue to live eternally and become a celestial human, or condemned and thrown alive into the lake of fire, suffering a second death. However, we who are already celestial humans will not face judgment at that time. As Jesus said:

Amp Jn 5:24 *I assure you, most solemnly I tell you, the person whose ears are open to My words [who listens to My message] and believes and trusts in and clings to and relies on Him Who sent Me has (possesses now) eternal life. And he does not come into judgment [does not incur sentence of judgment, will not come under condemnation], but he has already passed over out of death into life.*

All this is bestowed upon us, those who love and believe Jesus—we who possess His Spirit and worship Him in both Spirit and in truth. As it has been said:

Amp 1Co 2:9 *But, on the contrary, as the Scripture says, What eye has not seen and ear has not heard and has not entered into the heart of man, [all that] God has prepared (made and keeps ready) for those who love Him [who hold Him in affectionate reverence, promptly obeying Him and gratefully recognizing the benefits He has bestowed].*

Amp 1Co 2:10 *Yet to us God has unveiled and revealed them by and through His Spirit, for the [Holy] Spirit searches diligently, exploring and examining everything, even sounding the profound and bottomless things of God [the divine counsels and things hidden and beyond man's scrutiny].*

Amp 1Co 2:11 *For what person perceives (knows and understands) what passes through a man's thoughts except the man's own spirit within him? Just so no one discerns (comes to know and comprehend) the thoughts of God except the Spirit of God.*

Amp 1Co 2:12 *Now we have not received the spirit [that belongs to] the world, but the [Holy] Spirit Who is from God, [given to us] that we might realize and comprehend and appreciate the gifts [of divine favor and blessing so freely and lavishly] bestowed on us by God.*

Amp 1Co 2:13 And we are setting these truths forth in words not taught by human wisdom but taught by the [Holy] Spirit, combining and interpreting spiritual truths with spiritual language [to those who possess the Holy Spirit].

Amp 1Co 2:14 But the natural, nonspiritual man does not accept or welcome or admit into his heart the gifts and teachings and revelations of the Spirit of God, for they are folly (meaningless nonsense) to him; and he is incapable of knowing them [of progressively recognizing, understanding, and becoming better acquainted with them] because they are spiritually discerned and estimated and appreciated.

Amp 1Co 2:15 But the spiritual man tries all things [he examines, investigates, inquires into, questions, and discerns all things], yet is himself to be put on trial and judged by no one [he can read the meaning of everything, but no one can properly discern or appraise or get an insight into him].

Amp 1Co 2:16 For who has known or understood the mind (the counsels and purposes) of the Lord so as to guide and instruct Him and give Him knowledge? But we have the mind of Christ (the Messiah) and do hold the thoughts (feelings and purposes) of His heart.

We must keep in mind the importance of the words highlighted in verse 9. It is true that in the beginning our default world view and reflex response to everything is to see, understand, and act out of the wisdom of this world, the wisdom of the spirit of Adam—the spirit wisdom we were born with. However, the gift of God is so valuable, even life changing, that we have an obligation to impose upon ourselves to view, understand and act out of the spirit wisdom given to us through the death of Jesus. Until His Spirit wisdom becomes our default understanding, we must humble and discipline ourselves, no matter how tempting and natural it feels to see things through the wisdom of this world. In this way only, can we grow in union with Christ, and learn to worship Him in spirit and in truth.

NIV Ro 8:5 Those who live according to the sinful nature have their minds set on what that nature desires; but those who live in accordance with the Spirit have their minds set on what the Spirit desires.

NIV Ro 8:6 The mind of sinful man is death, but the mind controlled by the Spirit is life and peace;

NIV Ro 8:7 the sinful mind is hostile to God. It does not submit to God's law, nor can it do so.

NIV Ro 8:8 Those controlled by the sinful nature cannot please God.

NIV Ro 8:9 You, however, are controlled not by the sinful nature but by the Spirit, if the Spirit of God lives in you. And if anyone does not have the Spirit of Christ, he does not belong to Christ.

NIV Ro 8:10 But if Christ is in you, your body is dead because of sin, yet your spirit is alive because of righteousness.

NIV Ro 8:11 And if the Spirit of him who raised Jesus from the dead is living in you, he who raised Christ from the dead will also give life to your mortal bodies through his Spirit, who lives in you.

NIV Ro 8:12 Therefore, brothers, we have an obligation—but it is not to the sinful nature, to live according to it.

NIV Ro 8:13 For if you live according to the sinful nature, you will die; but if by the Spirit you put to death the misdeeds of the body, you will live,

NIV Ro 8:14 because those who are led by the Spirit of God are sons of God.

NIV Ro 8:15 For you did not receive a spirit that makes you a slave again to fear, but you received the Spirit of sonship. And by him we cry, "Abba, Father."

NIV Ro 8:16 The Spirit himself testifies with our spirit that we are God's children.

NIV Ro 8:17 Now if we are children, then we are heirs—heirs of God and co-heirs with Christ, if indeed we share in his sufferings in order that we may also share in his glory.

. . . Amen

Notes

[2] Meek. In *Merriam Webster*, Retrieved May 2016, from www.merriam-webster.com/dictionary/meek

Bibliography

Amplified Bible. Scripture quotations marked (AMP) are taken from the Amplified Bible, Copyright © 1954, 1958, 1962, 1964, 1965, 1987 by The Lockman Foundation. Used by permission.

Good News Translation (Today's English Version, Second Edition). Scripture quotations marked (GNT) are from the Good News Translation in Today's English Version- Second Edition, Copyright © 1992 by American Bible Society. Used by Permission.

New American Standard. Scripture quotations marked (NAS) are taken from the NEW AMERICAN STANDARD BIBLE®, Copyright © 1960,1962,1963,1968,1971,1972,1973,1975,1977,1995 by The Lockman Foundation. Used by permission.

New International Version. Scriptures taken from the Holy Bible, New International Version®, NIV®. Copyright © 1973, 1978, 1984 by Biblica, Inc.™ Used by permission of Zondervan. All rights reserved worldwide. www.zondervan.com The "NIV" and "New International Version" are trademarks registered in the United States Patent and Trademark Office by Biblica, Inc.™

New Living Translation. Holy Bible, New Living Translation copyright © 1996, 2004, 2007 by Tyndale House Foundation. Used by permission of Tyndale House Publishers Inc., Carol Stream, Illinois 60188. All rights reserved. New Living, NLT, and the New Living Translation logo are registered` trademarks of Tyndale House Publishers.

Melani Pyke. *Jesus as Teacher (The Sermon on the Mount)*. Retrieved from http://melpyke.com/workszoom/1954705

World English Bible. Scripture quotations marked (WEB) are taken from The World English Bible, which is in the public domain. Special thanks to Michael Paul Johnson and all who worked on the translation as a means to release a modern version of the Bible that is available for non-copyright use. A reminder that the Bible is   not owned by man.

ABOUT THE AUTHORS

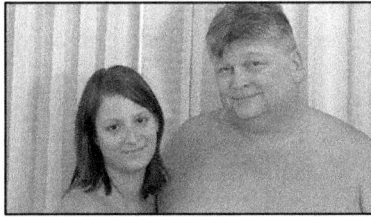

We are just a voice

WEB Jn 1:19 *This is John's testimony* (about himself), *when the Jews sent priests and Levites from Jerusalem to ask him, "Who are you?"*
WEB Jn 1:20 *He declared, and didn't deny, but he declared, "I am not the Christ."*
WEB Jn 1:21 *They asked him, "What then? Are you Elijah?"*
He said, "I am not."
"Are you the prophet?"
He answered, "No."
WEB Jn 1:22 *They said therefore to him, "Who are you? Give us an answer to take back to those who sent us. What do you say about yourself?"*
WEB Jn 1:23 *He said, "__I am the voice__ of one crying in the wilderness, 'Make straight the way of the Lord . . ."*

True prophets in the Bible did not convince people who they were; in fact, they refused to talk about themselves. They refused to bring credibility to the words of God they spoke by trying to get people to believe who they were and trust them. They knew that it would be profaning the words of God to do so, and it would be elevating themselves above God's words. They knew that God's words have their own credibility because they are from God. And God will show them (His own words) as from Him.

God's prophets also knew that those who truly love God will, therefore, benefit from their words, and those who are lovers of themselves will not benefit from them, because they will be dismissive and not trust them. The time is over that we look at the person who speaks to decide if we believe. We must begin to discern if the words are from God and if they carry God's Spirit.

You might say to that, "but not everyone can discern God." If that is the case, then they indict themselves as not being "known" by Jesus. They unwittingly reveal about themselves that they desire to do their own will and not the Lord's, just as the religious leaders who wanted Jesus to prove His credibility so they could decide if His words were from God.

Amp Jn 7:16 *Jesus answered them by saying, My teaching is not My own, but His Who sent Me.*
Amp Jn 7:17 *If any man desires to do His will (God's pleasure), he will know (have the needed illumination to recognize, and can tell for himself) whether the teaching is from God or whether I am speaking from Myself and of My own accord and on My own authority.*

Many will think this is an oversimplified notion. However, it is so simple that it is not only true but reveals a simple but foundational truth about the person. What Jesus is saying is that if a man has a pure heart and wants to do the will of God above his own will, then what seems intuitively right (what sets well with that man) will be God's will and His words. However, even if you are a scholar, theologian, or work in the field of religion, and you desire to carry out your own will, having your own agendas and ambitions, well then, what seems right to that man is not God's will or His words, but that which lines up with his own will.

Generally speaking, the greatest religious minds in the world judge if something is from God by looking at the standing and qualifications of the man speaking them. In the above case, Jesus shows they may be smart in their own eyes, believing they know what is from God and therefore able to judge according to their knowledge of God. However, that would be saying in effect, we know everything about God because of our great knowledge. Therefore, if you say anything outside of our knowledge of God, or outside of the knowledge base of the accepted theological models, or if you are not a qualified student of those accepted models, then we must deduce your words are not from God.

To Jesus, they show about themselves that they don't recognize His words as from God because of their personal acquaintance with God. Instead, they have to judge by facts. They show themselves as having no real relationship with God; they would not recognize Him when He stands right before them. As a matter of fact, on another occasion when they showed contempt for Him, Jesus said of them:

NIV Jn 5:42 *. . . but I know you. I know that you do not have the love of God in your hearts.*

They were once again wanting Him to prove who He was, and what right He had to talk the way He did. Jesus, instead of being intimidated, marveled at how He spoke and acted out everything the Father willed, yet they did not recognize His words as His Father's. Furthermore, they were, by nature, hostile and offended towards those words.

Let's look at that closer through an illustration. For example, you have a woman who claims to be married to a man named Jim. Then, a man claiming to be Jim and her husband approaches her. The above case is like the wife doubting this man is her husband. So then, she begins to question him. For example, "If you're Jim, when were you born?" And, "What kind of car did you have when you first got your license?" If he doesn't answer to her satisfaction, she decides that he is not her husband Jim. This might seem reasonable, and if he got the answers incorrect or didn't remember, the people listening might believe her when she says, "this is not my husband."

If there was anybody in the crowd that had wisdom, they might say this begs another question, "Hey lady, are you really Jim's wife or are you an imposter?" The reasoning of the wise man is, do you really need factual evidence to know if he is your husband? Don't you know your husband when he is standing right in front of you? Jesus is marveling at the religious leaders who are supposed to know God and claim to be in union with Him. However, they don't recognize Him when He stands before them. They don't even recognize His words as from God. Do they really need factual evidence to know something that they are supposed to have intimate knowledge of? Next question, why does it not occur to anyone to question if these men of God, leaders of the Jewish faith, may be imposters because they don't judge if someone and their words are from God by their intimate knowledge of God? They need factual evidence?

What did that tell Jesus? It told Him that even the top religious leaders who know the written word by heart can't recognize God when they stand right in front of Him. It told Him that they were, in their inner man, hostile and threatened by God's words. It told Him that, in their inner selves, they really had no love or even any natural attraction towards God, His heart, and the Spirit of His words. They were obviously naturally repelled by them; they had no real love for God and their response showed it. However, to the religious leaders, they thought themselves wise and discerning to hold Jesus and His words suspect by judging Him with factual evidence. How disappointing it must have been to Jesus that the best of the best had no intimate knowledge of God and they were repulsed by Him when facing Him. Yes, Jesus' deduction was correct, there was no love of God in their hearts.

It is a Biblical fact that the major way we will be judged is it will be proven if we have a natural attraction to please God and do His will, therefore saying about us that we love Him more than ourselves. Learning by the folly of the leaders and the scholarly of Jesus' day, it is not by a knowledgeable and scholarly mind that one can successfully judge or discern what words coming from what person are from God or not. You can't judge superficially. No, it takes something much greater than to know every Bible verse by heart and to be able to have insightful knowledge of the person speaking them. It actually takes something much harder to attain than perfect scholarly knowledge of the written word. It takes a pure heart. Not meaning a sinless heart, but one which is single-minded, wanting to please God by serving Him and wanting to do His will at the expense of their own. This is what qualifies one to recognize if something is from God.

WEB Mt 5:8 *Blessed are the pure in heart, for they shall see God.*

It is true that as Colleen and I gain a larger following of our teachings and ministry, people will undoubtedly come to know us personally, and what kind of people we are. However, as teachers, we teach people how to live as spiritual men and women, discerning life in a spiritual way.

We have found the best way to teach discerning of spirit. It is not by knowing how to figure people out or to train them to have a spiritual power. No, we teach them to be single-minded when it comes to God, to be surrendered to His will in a pure or holistic way.

Having a still spirit which is not agitated with passions will create a huge contrast. The contrast of having the stillness of God's Spirit rule your heart coming in contact with the agitated spirit energies the people of this world operate out of makes one sensitive to discern spirit.

Jesus was right; wanting to do God's will with all your heart alone will cause you to recognize if one has God's Spirit in them and if they speak word's which are from God. As the saying goes, "You can't cheat an honest man."

NIV Jn 8:15 *You judge by human standards...*

NIV Jn 7:24 *Stop judging by mere appearances, and make a right judgment."*

As such, Colleen and I would like to be known first as a voice, just a voice. We want the words we speak from God to have more prominence and have their own credibility, than that of who we are. Therefore, we don't want to propagate people judging superficially if one is from God by giving our Bio. We want the words we speak to be more important than who we are. We want those who have a pure heart in wanting to serve God to check in their heart if we and the words we speak are from God.

We want those who don't have a pure heart to have a change of heart so they may know for themselves the voice and words of God when they hear them. However, we want to point people in the way to properly discern so they may know for themselves if we are from God and speak His words; in the same way John the Baptist tried to convey. You ask about us, and we will tell you about Him. You insist on wanting to know about us, and we will then tell you, we are just a voice making way for the One you should know and should be asking about. We are not a face or a name or people you should want to know, we are just a voice which gives voice to the One whose words you need to know.

OTHER BOOKS BY THE NAKED APOSTLES

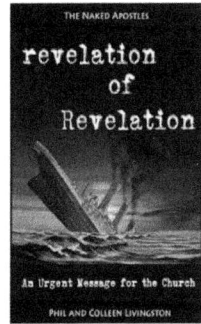

For ordering information please visit our website at
www.nakedapostles.org